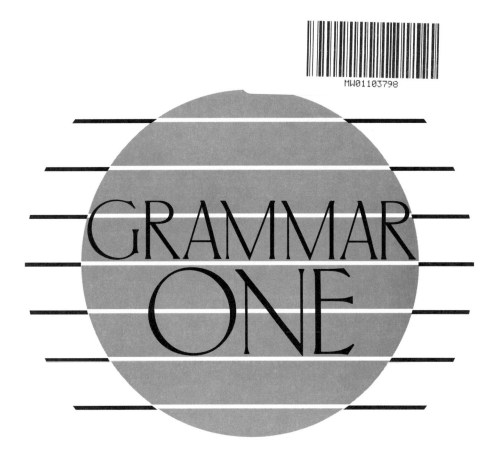

GRAMMAR ONE

Jean Zukowski/Faust
and
Mary Kay O'Brien

Northern Arizona State University

MAXWELL MACMILLAN
INTERNATIONAL PUBLISHING GROUP
New York Oxford Singapore Sydney
COLLIER MACMILLAN CANADA
Toronto

Executive Editor: Mary Jane Peluso
Editor: Maggie Barbieri
Managing Editor: Jennifer Carey

This book was set in Caslon by Progressive Typographers, Inc.,
printed and bound by Viking Press.
The cover was printed by Viking Press.

Library of Congress Cataloging-in-Publication Data

Zukowski/Faust, Jean.
Grammar one / Jean Zukowski/Faust and Mary Kay O'Brien.
p. cm.
ISBN 0-02-336480-7
1. English language—Textbooks for foreign speakers. 2. English language—Grammar—1950- I. O'Brien, Mary Kay. II. Title.
PE1128.Z84 1991
428.2'4—dc20 90-43780
CIP

Collier Macmillan Canada
1200 Eglinton Avenue, E.
Don Mills, Ontario, M3C 3N1

Printing: 1 2 3 4 5 6 7 Year: 1 2 3 4 5 6 7

Maxwell Macmillan International Publishing Group
ESL/EFL Dept.
866 Third Avenue
New York, NY 10022

Printed in the U.S.A.

ISBN 0-02-336480-7

To all students of
international English,
our shared language.

Introduction

Grammar One is a textbook for the beginning English language student. With a grammar base, using simple explanations and minimal prose, this text uses a controlled vocabulary, a progressive approach to structures, and many visual cues for meaning — all within the context of an American community, Springfield.

The unique features of *Grammar One* all center on and emanate from the context.

Real language use stems from human interaction. The community of Springfield, with residents of all ages (children, teenagers, young adults, tradespeople, professional people, and retired people), is the surface focus of the text. Situations and personalities are interwoven to create a fabric of real life in a multiple-strand story. Thus, using the best principles of today's communicative methods in presentation, *Grammar One* answers teachers' and students' needs for an English text with community-based language needs and a class text and workbook combination.

New words are introduced in easily understood social frameworks. Line drawings and scenes closely related to the situations in the exercises help students figure out the meanings of words and the dynamics of the use of those new words.

Structures, beginning with BE, are introduced in groups; before a new structure is taught, it does not appear in exercise directions or grammar explanations. For this reason, charts are used to present grammatical forms, and summary charts are added to help students connect elements that they have learned and to provide easy reference. This grading of structures and control of vocabulary is also the reason for the limited language of the grammar notes. The authors believe that the language of the grammatical explanations must be within the scope of the student. The student can work through the text alone if he or she so desires. The role of the teacher in the classroom becomes more important as no text can provide the animated multi-sensory explication of grammar that a teacher at a chalkboard can provide.

Exercises are plentiful and focused. In general, a teacher will find that there is an exercise following each grammar point that requires only the incorporation and repetition of the lesson, with minimal new information. Next come progressively more integrated exercises, with earlier grammar points recycled and reinforced. The teacher will find exercises for both class work and homework assignment.

Exercises are contexts within themselves. Each exercise is a situation in the lives of the people of Springfield. Even at the beginning of *Grammar One,* with limited language and only one structure, an attempt has been made to keep to the principle that all language in the text be accessible to the true beginning student. Items within some exercises are short contexts (mini-contexts) to help students learn the scope of the words and structures by working through the many short contexts and having to manipulate the language within them.

The index is an easy reference tool for both teacher and student.

The *Grammar One* presentation, with pictures and a developing story-like community, with boxes for charts and grammar explanations, with two-color printing, with extras like maps and posters, with tapes and variety within a usable workbook format, is different and up to date.

Grammar One is the text to use to start learning English as it is truly a beginning grammar book. It does not overwhelm the student; it is ultimately adaptable and well-indexed. Teachers can pick and choose exercises that relate to the students' lives and needs, or they can lead the class through the whole text as the main text, or with the text as a supplementary text. In either case, *Grammar One* is easily adapted to the needs of the beginning English language student.

Contents

Unit 1: The Verb BE

LET'S BEGIN!

1.1 Subject + BE + Noun

Taylor College
Hi! I am Ann Clark. This is Bill. We are friends.
Yes, I'm Bill Henderson. We're students at Taylor College.

Who/What	BE	Who/What
I	am	Ann Clark.
We	are	friends.

Who/What	BE		Who/What
You	are		Ted.
You	are		student.
What	is	your	name?

Who/What	BE		Who/What
That	is		Joe.
He	is	a good	friend.

Hi, Joe.
Hi! This is Kate. She's a new student.

Who/What	BE		Who/What
This	is		Kate.
She	is	a new	student.

Good morning, class.
I am Dr. Hunter.
This is my Math 100 class.
You are my students.
Let's begin.
Who is that?
That's Dr. Hunter.
He's a good teacher.
They are lucky students!

Who/What	BE		Who/What
You	are	my	students.
They	are	lucky	students.
Who	is		that?
What	is		that?

Summary

Who/What	BE		Adjective	Who/What
I	am	a		student.
We	are			students.
You (one)	are	my		friend.
You (many)	are			beginners.
He	is	a	good	friend.
She	is	a	new	student.
They	are		lucky	students.
This	is			Kate.
That	is			Joe.
Who	is			that?
What	is	your		name?

Note: *This* and *that* are indefinite pronouns. *This* points to someone or something close by. *That* points to someone or something that is not close by. *This* and *that* can take the place of the subject. *What* and *who* are also pronouns. They make questions. *Who* refers to people. *What* refers to things, even things about people, like their names.

Exercise 1 Dr. Hunter's Math 100 Class.

Use the verb BE.

1. Ann Clark ________ a student in Dr. Hunter's Math 100 class.
2. Ann and Bill Henderson ________ friends.
3. They ________ students at Taylor College.
4. Ann: Ted, ________ you a student in my math class too?
5. This ________ Kate. She ________ a new student.
6. Dr. Hunter: This ________ my Math 100 class. You ________ my students.
7. That ________ Dr. Hunter. He ________ a good teacher.
8. They ________ lucky students.

Exercise 2 Meet Some People. Mini-Contexts.

Use the verb BE *in these sentences.*

1. Dr. Hunter:		I ________ your teacher. My name ________ Dr. Hunter.
2. Bill:		That ________ Ted. He ________ a student in my math class.
	Ann:	Who ________ that?
	Bill:	That ________ Kate. She ________ a student in math class too.
3. Ted:		Who ________ that?
	Bill:	That ________ Dr. Hunter. He ________ a math teacher.
	Ted:	________ he a good teacher?
	Bill:	Yes, he is.
4. Ted:		Dr. Hunter ________ a good teacher.
	Kate:	We ________ lucky.
5. Ann:		What ________ your name?
	Kate:	I ________ Kate Dowling.
	Ann:	I'm glad to meet you. My name ________ Ann Clark.
6. Bill:		Hi, I ________ Bill Henderson. What ________ your name?
	Ted:	Ted Johnson. ________ you in my math class?
	Bill:	Yes! I am.

Exercise 3 Who Are Your Classmates?

Ask and learn their names. Work with a partner. Learn his or her name. Learn something about your partner. Introduce your partner to the rest of the class.

Example: This is my new friend, Ann Clark. She is a new student.

____

____

Note to Teacher: One student asks the others "Who is that?" pointing to students around the room. When this exercise is finished, put students in groups of three. Have student A ask student B the name of student C and answer to practice "He is . . . /She is. . . ."

1.2 {Pronoun/Noun} + BE + Adjective (+ Noun)

I'm Tom Turner.
I'm tall.
I'm a good student.
I'm strong.
I'm brave.
I'm a football player.

Subject	BE	Adjective	Noun
I	am		Tom Turner.
I	am	tall.	
I	am	a good	student.

Exercise 4 Who Is That?

Use the BE verb in the blanks to complete the sentences.

Ann: Who ________ that?

Bill: That ________ Tom Turner.

Ann: He ________ tall.

Bill: Yes, and he ________ strong and brave. He ________ a good football player.

Exercise 5 Talk About Yourself.

Complete the sentences.

Example: My name is Kate. I am a new student.

My name is ________________. I am ________________ and ________ ________.

Exercise 6 Talk About a Classmate.

Examples: This is Betty. She is a Canadian. This is Tom. He is tall.

This is ________________. He/She is ________________.

Exercise 7 Talk About a Member of Your Family.
(mother, father, sister, brother)

Example: This is Pam Clark. She's my mother.

This is ____________________. He/She is ____________________.

1.3 Noun + BE + NOT + Adjective (+ Noun)

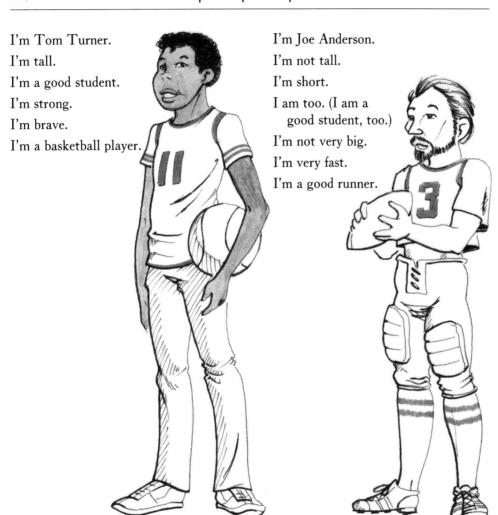

I'm Tom Turner.
I'm tall.
I'm a good student.
I'm strong.
I'm brave.
I'm a basketball player.

I'm Joe Anderson.
I'm not tall.
I'm short.
I am too. (I am a good student, too.)
I'm not very big.
I'm very fast.
I'm a good runner.

NOTE: *Too* means *also* (the same thing, not different).

Subject Noun	BE	NOT	Adjective	Noun
I	am	not	tall.	
I	am	not	very big.	
I	am	not	a	football player.

Exercise 8 Joe Anderson.

Use BE *and* NOT *to complete the sentences.*

Joe Anderson __is not__ a basketball player. He ________ tall. He ________ very big, but he is very strong. Tom Turner ________ a runner. He ________ small.

Exercise 9 Talk About Yourself.

My name is ________________. I am not ________________.

Exercise 10 Talk About a Classmate.

This is ________________. He/She is not ________________.

Exercise 11 Talk About a Member of Your Family. *(father, mother, sister, brother)*

This is ________. He/She is not ________.

1.4 Possessive Adjectives *(my, our, your, his, her, their)*

Jane: Let's go to the gym.
Joe: OK.
Jane: Let's put our stuff here.
Joe: Here is my backpack.
Jane: Here is my jacket.
Here are our towels.
Here is your bag.
Joe: What's that?
Jane: That's Jack's bag. And here is his towel. This is Ann's bag. Here are her shoes.
Joe: Where's Jack?
Jane: Here he is!
Jack: Where are Ann and Bill?
Jane: They are at the student union, but their stuff is here.
Joe: Let's go. Let's meet them at the gym.

Summary

I ⟶ my	Here is my backpack.
we ⟶ our	Here are our towels.
you ⟶ your	Here is your towel. (one person)
	Here are your towels. (many people)
he ⟶ his	Here is his towel.
she ⟶ her	Here are her shoes.
they ⟶ their	Here is their stuff.

Exercise 12 Jack and Jane Are at the Gym.

Use my, our, your, her, his *or* their *to complete the dialogue. The subject pronouns* (I, you, he, she, we, they) *can help you.*

Jane: Where is ________ jacket? (I)

Jack: Here it is.

Jane: Oh, thanks. Where is ________ bag? (you)

Jack: It's here. And here is Joe's backpack and ________ towel. (he)

Jane: Here are Ann and Bill, and here is ________ stuff. (they)

Jack: This is Ann's bag, and here are ________ shoes. (she)

Exercise 13 Whose? Mini-Contexts.

Use the possessive adjective.

1. Ann: That's the new student.
   Bill: What's ________ name?
   Ann: Beth, I think.
2. Beth: Hi, ________ name is Beth Parker. What's ________ name?
   Peggy: ________ name is Peggy.
   Beth: What's ________ last name?
   Peggy: Smith.

3. Ann: Are you ready for ________ math class?
   Bill: Yes, I have ________ books and ________ paper.
   Ann: Do you have ________ calculator?
   Bill: No. I don't have one.
4. Joe: Hi, Tom. Who's ________ friend?
   Tom: This is ________ friend Mike. He's in ________ math class. Mike, this is ________ friend, Joe.
   Joe: Nice to meet you.
5. Mr. Smith: Where's ________ car?
   Mrs. Smith: The Clarks have it. ________ car is at the garage.
6. This is a picture of ___my___ family. ________ mother is Pamela Clark. ________ father's name is Ed. We live in Springfield. ________ house is on Oak Street. We have a dog. ________ name is Spot. ________ cat is Fluffy.

1.5 LET'S + Verb + Rest of the Sentence

LET'S + Verb + Rest of the Sentence		
Let's	go	
Let's	go	now!
Let's	put	our stuff here.
Let's	meet	them at the gym.

Exercise 14 Let's Go to the Lake!

Use LET'S *and one of these expressions to finish the dialogue.*

go swimming	lie on the sand	get a soda	buy a hot dog
go for a walk	get a hamburger	play volleyball	get some ice cream

1. Joe I'm hungry. Let's ________.
   Jack: I'm not hungry. Let's ________.

2. Ann: I'm hot. Let's ________.
   Jane: I'm not. Let's ________.

3. Joe: I'm thirsty. Let's ________.
   Barbara: I'm hungry too. Let's ________.

4. Bob: I'm bored. Let's ________.
   Kate: OK. Let's go.

Exercise 15 A Sale at the Mall. Mini-Contexts.

Here is an advertising sheet from the mall. It is like a newspaper. There are many sales today. The prices are very good. Complete the dialogues with Let's. *Use expressions like these:* look at the ads, buy new pants, go to Fancy Shoes, look at dresses at Martin's, try on clothes at the Clothes Line, stop at the Hanger, see the shirts at L & J's. *The first one is done for you.*

1.	Peggy Smith:	These shoes are really old, Mom.
	Emily Smith:	*Let's go to Wilson's Shoes*.
2.	Pamela Clark:	There is a sale at the mall. Dresses are on sale at Martin's.
	Ann Clark:	________________.
	Pamela Clark:	OK. Let's go.
3.	Jane:	Where is the sale on skirts?
	Kate:	The Hanger. ________________.
	Jane:	No, let's not. ________________.
	Kate:	No, ________________.
	Jane:	Let's go different places.
	Kate:	That's a good idea.
4.	Tom:	Where are the best sales?
	Joe:	________________ to get sweaters.
	Tom:	OK. . . . My pants are old.
	Joe:	________________ to get new pants.
	Tom:	OK. . . . My shoes are really bad.
	Joe:	________________.
	Tom:	OK. Let's go!
5.	Beth:	I need a new shirt.
	Peggy:	________________.
	Beth:	What do you need? I need everything. ________ ________ for sweaters.
6.	Ann:	I need some shoes, Mom.
	Pam:	OK. ________________ on the sheet. What is a good buy?
	Ann:	________________. All summer shoes are half off. (50%)

Unit 2: BE and Adverbs of Place

WHERE ARE WE?

2.1 BE + Adverbs of Place

Example Sentences in Context:

I am here alone.
The movie theater is downtown. My friends are there.
My radio is at home. It is on the table.
The pizza place is at the mall. My friends are there.
The bookstore is in the city. It is uptown.
The ice cream shop is on the other side of town.
There is nothing here, but I am here.
My friends are all somewhere. But I am here.
Where are they?

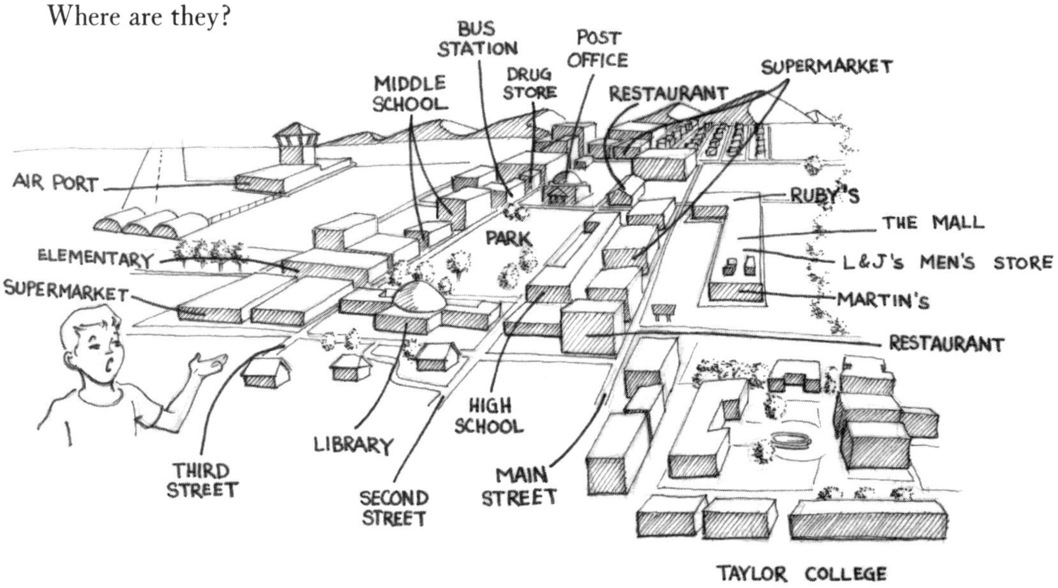

Subject	BE	Adverbs of Place
I	am	here.
My friends	are	there.
Beth	is	downtown/uptown.
John	is	home.
Tom	is	at home too.
John and Tom	are	at home.
They	are	at home.
My radio	is	on the table at home.
She	is	on the other side of the river.
They	are	somewhere.
They	are	where? = Where are they?

Note: Some adverbs of place are just one word. Some are phrases, or several words. These phrases use a preposition (*at, on, of, in*) and a noun. These phrases are prepositional phrases (*at the mall, on the table*). Ten words in English can show place without a preposition: *here, there, somewhere, downtown, uptown, downstairs, upstairs, outside, inside,* and *home*. *Home* can be used with *at* too: *She is (at) home.*

2.2 Prepositional Phrases as Adverbs of Place

Some adverbs of place are single words: *here, there, somewhere, downtown, uptown, home.* Some adverbs of place are phrases (Preposition + Noun): *at the bookstore, at home, on the table, in the city.*

Preposition	+ Noun
in	a country *(in the US)*
	a closed place *(in the closet)*
	a small vehicle *(in a car)*
	inside a limited place *(in jail)*
	a situation *(in trouble)*
at	a location *(at the mall)*
	an address *(at 112 Main Street)*
on	a side *(on the left)*
	a street *(on Park Street)*
	a large vehicle *(on the train)*
	top of a small vehicle like a bicycle *(on his bicycle)*
	top of a smooth surface *(on the table)*
	the floor of a building *(on the top floor)*

Exercise 1 At the Beach

Complete the sentences with adverbs. Use single words like here *or prepositions like* at *and* in.

It's summer time. No one is here with me. Where is everyone? I am ________ the lake ________ the beach ________ the sand. Ann is ________ an airplane to Chicago. Barbara is ________ the air. Joe is ________ the water. Ted is ________ the sand. John is ________ New York. Bob is ________ the hot dog stand. Bill and Jim are ________ a boat. Sally is ________ a motorcycle.

Exercise 2 At School. Mini-Contexts.

Complete the sentences with adverbs. Use single words like here *or prepositions like* at *and* in.

1. Jim is a student ________ this school. He is ________ now. He is ________ Room 200. He is ________ class from 9:00 until 3:00.
2. Jane's house is ________ Second Street. It's ________ 100 Second Street, but Jane isn't ________ home now. She is ________ New York.
3. Mark is not ________ class. He is not ________ the bookstore. He is not ________ the mall. He is not ________ the library. Mark is ________ home now.
4. Ann: Jill and Bob are not ________. They are ________ a party ________ Mark's house.

   Bill: The party is not ________ Mark's house. It is ________ a big room ________ a hotel ________ First Street.
5. Jane: Where are your books?

   Kate: They are ________ a box ________ a table ________ my room.

   Jane: Let's get them.

   Kate: OK. Let's go.

6. Jane: Where is Jim now?
Jack: I don't know. Do you?
Jane: Yes, Jim is ________ an airplane now. He is ________ a first class seat.

7. Joe: Where are our friends?
Tom: They are ________ somewhere, but they are not ________ here.

8. May: Where is my coat?
Pam: It is ________ a closet ________ the end of the hall.

9. George: Where is the telephone?
Ed: It is ________ a small table ________ the kitchen.
George: Where is the telephone book?
Ed: ________ the drawer ________ the table.

10. Beth: Where is his house?
Bob: It is ________ 1600 Pennsylvania Avenue.
Beth: ________ what city?
Bob: ________ Washington, DC.

Exercise 3 At the Department Store.

Add the prepositions.

This is the elevator at Ruby's Department store.
The store is ________ 808 South Broadway.
The elevator is ________ the middle of the store.

This is the sign by the elevator:

RUBY'S DEPARTMENT STORE

DEPARTMENT	FLOOR
CAFETERIA	LOWER LEVEL 1
CHILDREN'S CLOTHES	FIRST FLOOR
CHILDREN'S TOYS	SECOND FLOOR
JEWELRY	FIRST FLOOR
LINENS	SECOND FLOOR
MEN'S CLOTHES	SECOND FLOOR
PARKING	LOWER LEVEL 2
PERFUME	FIRST FLOOR
SKY-VIEW RESTAURANT	ROOF

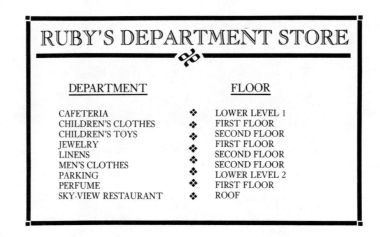

Help the elevator operator. Answer the questions.

1. Mrs. Clark: Where is Women's Clothes?
   Operator: ________________
2. Mrs. Smith: Where is the Linen department?
   Operator: ________________
3. Dr. Garcia: Where is Children's Toys?
   Operator: ________________
4. Kate: Where is the Perfume department?
   Operator: ________________
5. Mrs. Garcia: I want a new dress.
   Operator: Women's dresses are ________________
6. Sam: I want a watch band.
   Operator: Jewelry is ________________
7. Mrs. Wallace: I'm hungry. Where are the restaurants?
   Operator: ________________
8. Mrs. Clark: Where is my car?
   Operator: Parking is ________________

Exercise 4 Where Are the Houses of My Friends?

Add the prepositions to complete the sentences.

1. Jim's house is ___*at*___ 426 East First Street ___*in*___ Springfield.
2. Jim's place is ________ East First Street.
3. Jim's house is ________ the main street of town.
4. Tom's home is ________ the corner of First Street and Pine Avenue.
5. Judy's house is ________ San Francisco ________ Elm Street.
6. Mary's apartment is ________ Main Street ________ Toronto.
7. Tanya's home is ________ 2255 North High Street ________ downtown.
8. Mary's house is ________ 100 Park Street ________ Manhattan, Kansas, ________ the United States.
9. My house is ________ here. Where is your house?
10. My house is ________ there ________ the corner.

Exercise 5 Where Are the Students?

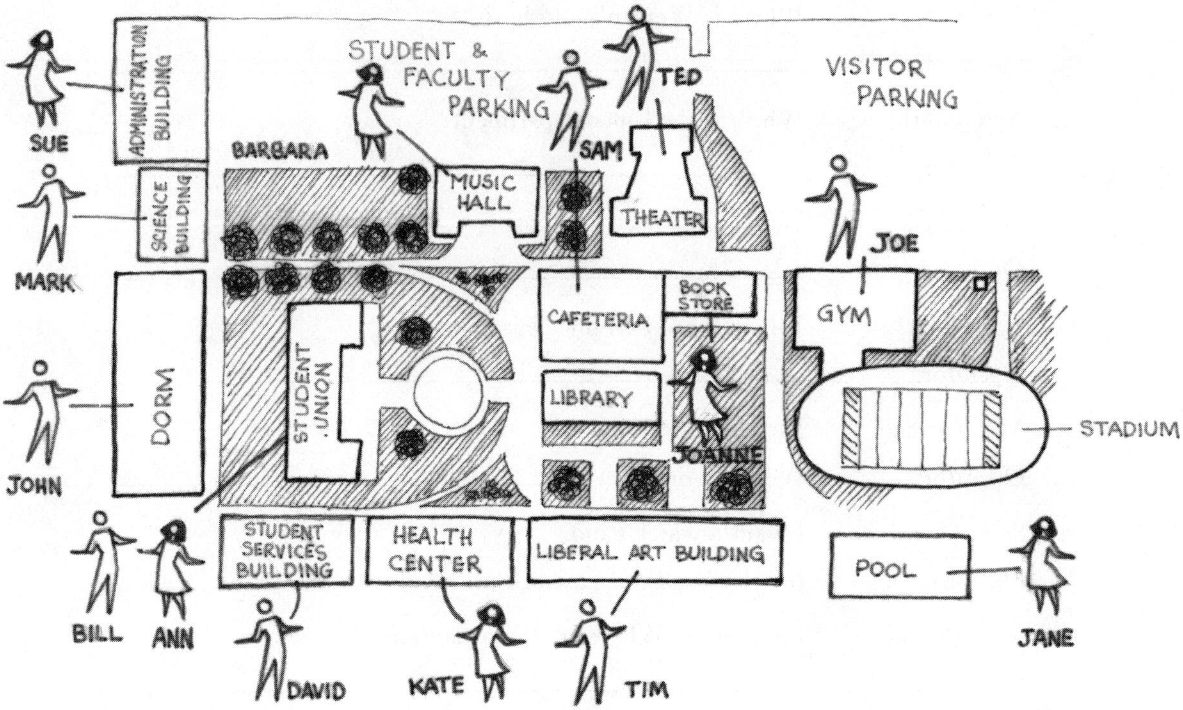

This is a map of campus. Where are the students? Use these expressions: at the Music Hall, at the cafeteria, at the Student Union, at the theater, at the gym, at the swimming pool, in the dorm, at the library, at the Liberal Arts Building, at the bookstore, at the Health Center, at the Administration Building, at the Student Services Building, at the Science Building, in the parking lot.

1. ____________ Jane? ____________
2. ____________ Mark? ____________
3. ____________ Barbara? ____________
4. ____________ John? ____________
5. ____________ Kate? ____________
6. ____________ Bill and Ann? ____________
7. ____________ Joe? ____________
8. ____________ Joanne? ____________
9. ____________ Sue? ____________
10. ____________ Sam? ____________
11. ____________ Ted? ____________
12. ____________ Tim? ____________
13. ____________ David? ____________

Exercise 6

Ask five of your classmates for their addresses. Write the answers.

Where is your house? ***My house is at 890 East David Drive.***

or ***It's on East David Drive.***

Where is your house? ______________________________

What is your address? ______________________________

Where is your house? ______________________________

Where do you live? ______________________________

What is your address? ______________________________

2.3 BE + Present Tense Adverbs of Time

Present tense uses these time words: *now, today, tonight, this morning, this afternoon, this evening.*

NOTE: Present tense verbs can mean future with present tense adverbs.

Example Sentences in Context:

All of my friends are at school now.

Tom is in class today.

This morning Joe is at the library. Ann is in the lab this morning.

There is a party tonight for Barbara. It is her birthday.

They are all ready for the party this evening.

When is the party? At seven o'clock.

Exercise 7 The Clarks' Schedules.

Ann Clark is a student at Taylor College. Her mother is a lawyer. Her name is Pamela Clark. Ann's father is a professor. His name is Edward J. Clark. They are busy people. They plan their time carefully. A time plan is a schedule. These are their schedules.

Ann's Schedule
This Week

	A.M.	P.M.
MON	class	tennis class 3:00
TUE	lab	work at the cafeteria 3 – 8
WED	class	library
THU	lab	3 – 8 work at the cafeteria 7:00 Barbara's birthday party
FRI	class	1:00 shopping at mall
SAT	workout 11:00 at the gym	football game with Bill
SUN	church	12:00 picnic with Smiths

Ann's Schedule
Next Week

	A.M.	P.M.
MON	class	3:00 tennis club
TUE	lab	work at the cafeteria 3 – 8
WED	class	library
THU	lab	work at the cafeteria 3 – 8
FRI	class	–
SAT	field trip with geology class all day →	
SUN	church	–

Pamela's Schedule
This Week

	A.M.	P.M.
MON	meeting with law firm partners	city hall
TUE	court	meet with client
WED	court	meet with Judge Davis
THU	meeting with client	workout at gym
FRI	city hall	1:00 shopping with Ann
SAT	gardening	dinner with Smiths
SUN	church	12:00 picnic with Smiths

Pamela's Schedule
Next Week

	A.M.	P.M.
MON	meeting with partners	meeting with client
TUE	court	meet with client
WED	court	city hall
THU	meeting at bank	workout at gym
FRI	go to State Capital for meeting	→
SAT	shopping	movie with Ed
SUN	Church	golf with Ed

Ed's Schedule
This Week

	A.M.	P.M.
MON	Class	office hours
TUE	Committee meeting	class
WED	class	office hours
THU	office hours	class
FRI	class	faculty meeting
SAT	yard work	dinner with Smiths
SUN	Church	12:00 picnic with Smiths

Ed's Schedule
Next Week

	A.M.	P.M.
MON	class	office hours
TUE	workout at gym	class
WED	class	office hours
THU	office hours	class
FRI	class	workout at gym
SAT	fishing	movie with Pam
SUN	Church	golf with Pam

Answer these questions about the Clarks' schedules.

1. When is Ann at the lab? ______
2. When is Ann's tennis class? ______
3. When is the shopping trip to the mall? ______
4. When is Pamela at city hall? (3 times) ______
5. What is on Ed's schedule next week on Saturday morning? ______
6. What is on Pamela's schedule this week on Wednesday afternoon? ______
7. When are Ed and Pam with Emily and George for dinner? ______
8. When are Ed, Pamela, and Ann with the Smiths? ______
9. When is golf on the schedule? ______
10. When is Pam at the State Capital? ______

Exercise 8

Ask a classmate some questions about the schedules.

______

______

______

______

Exercise 9 Your Schedule.

Write your own schedule here.

Schedule
This Week

	A.M.	P.M.
MON		
TUE		
WED		
THU		
FRI		
SAT		
SUN		

Schedule
Next Week

	A.M.	P.M.
MON		
TUE		
WED		
THU		
FRI		
SAT		
SUN		

Answer these questions about your schedule.

1. Where are you now? ______________________
2. What is on your schedule for this morning? ______________________
3. What is on your schedule tonight? ______________________
4. What is your plan for this afternoon? ______________________
5. What is on your schedule for this evening? ______________________

2.4 BE in the Past Tense (WAS and WERE)

Example Sentences in Context:

Yesterday was Tuesday.
It was a good day.
Last Tuesday was a good day too.
Jack was here last Tuesday morning.
That was a week ago.
Jack isn't here now.

Explanation:

Past tense = Verb + (past tense ending) + [time word or words]

BE + (past tense ending) = *was* or *were*

NOTE: BE is the most common verb in English. It is irregular (not regular). It has many different forms. In the past tense the form of BE is *was* for singular and *were* for plural—the past tense "ending" is not really an ending with the verb BE. It is part of these two words.

Examples of BE in the Past Tense in Context:

I am a student now. I *was* a student last year too.

Bill *is* a student in my math class this semester. He *was* a student at Taylor last semester too.

We *were* students together last semester. We are friends.

Bill and Ann are friends. They *were* in our math class too.

I am here now. +(past tense) = I *was* here then.

We are here now. +(past tense) = We *were* here then.

Exercise 10 Yesterday's Weather Map.

Look at the map. It is yesterday's weather map.

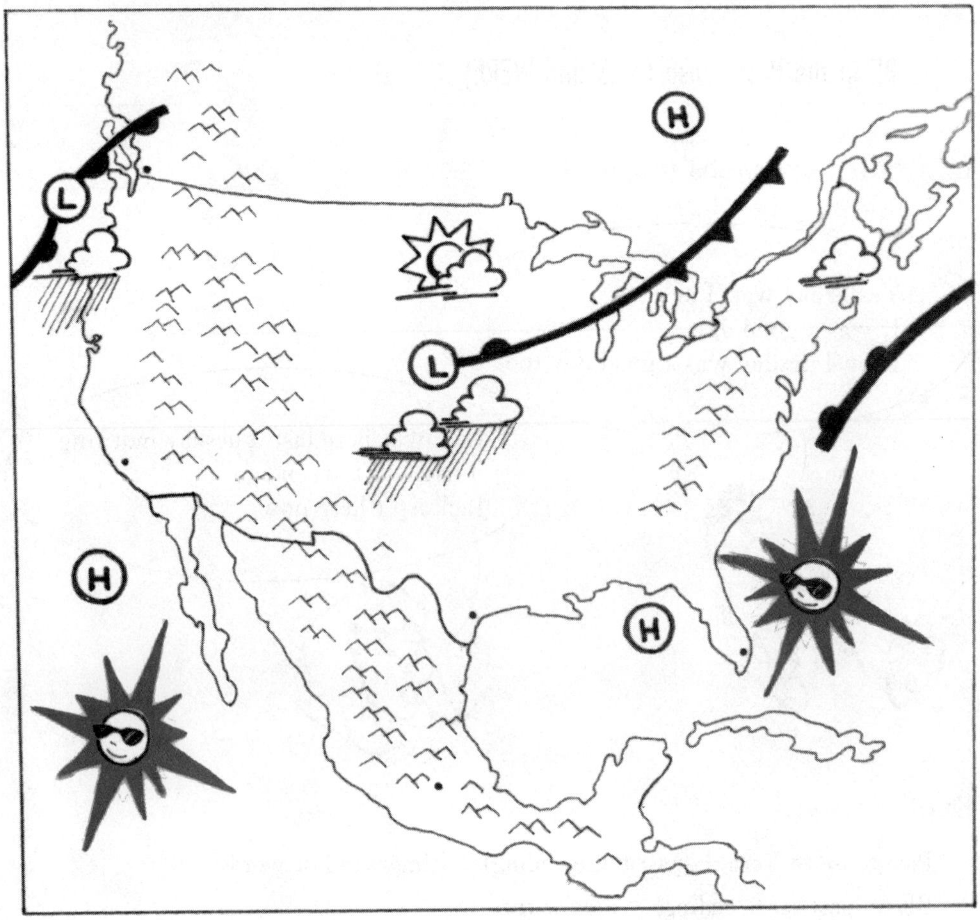

1. Where were there rainstorms? ____________
2. What was the weather in Miami? ____________
3. What was the weather in the mountains? ____________
4. Where was it sunny? ____________
5. How was the weather in New England? ____________
6. What was Vancouver's weather? ____________
7. What was the weather in Mexico City? ____________
8. How was the weather in Los Angeles? ____________

Exercise 11 In Class. Mini-Contexts.

Use WAS *or* WERE.

1. I am a student. I am at school now. Yesterday I ________ here. I am at school every day.

2. The students are really ready for the test today. Yesterday they ________ ready too, but the test ________ not. The test is ready now.

3. Ted is here now. His bus ________ not here an hour ago. It ________ late. His friends ________ here an hour ago, but they aren't here how. They are at school.

4. Jane: Where is the box of books? I can't find it.
   Kate: Here it is. It's here now, but it ________ not here an hour ago.

5. Joe: Where is my backpack?
   Tom: Isn't it on the table? It ________ there last night.
   Joe: Maybe it ________ there then, but it isn't there now.

6. Teacher: Where ________ you yesterday. You ________ not in class.
   Student: I ________ at home. I ________ sick, but I am not sick now.

Exercise 12 Where Were They Yesterday?

Finish the sentences with BE *verbs in present or past tense.*

Teacher: Our class ___*was*___ very small yesterday, and it ___*is*___ small today. Only you four students ___*are*___ here. Where ___*is*___ everyone today? Where ___*were*___ they yesterday?

1. Jim ________ at home today. He ________ in class yesterday.
2. I ________ here today, but I ________ sick yesterday, so I ________ at home.
3. Sue ________ in class yesterday, but she ________ at the doctor's office today.
4. Joe and Tom ________ in class today. They ________ in class yesterday too.
5. The teacher ________ in class today, and she ________ here yesterday too.
6. Yesterday David ________ in class, but today he ________ not.
7. Where ________ Barbara? She ________ here yesterday.
8. Where ________ you yesterday? ________ you here?

Exercise 13 She's at Home Today.

Practice with WAS *and* WERE. *Complete these mini-contexts with* BE *verbs in present and past tense.*

1. Ann is downtown today. She ________ at school yesterday.
2. Ted is a salesman. He is in Chicago today. He ________ in New York last week.
3. Pat is at work today. He ________ at work last night too.
4. Dan is in his office today. He ________ at home yesterday.

5. Jean is at City Hall this afternoon. This morning she ________ in her office.

6. Kate ________ at home today. She ________ at home yesterday too. She is sick. Jane ________ not sick today. She ________ sick last week.

7. Beth is at her sister's house today, but she ________ here yesterday.

8. Al is at school now, but he ________ in London last month.

9. Jan and Jean ________ here today. They ________ here every day last week too.

10. Joe and Tom ________ at the library today. They ________ there yesterday afternoon too.

11. The Clarks ________ at the store today, but they ________ home yesterday.

12. Mark is sick. He ________ home in bed now. He ________ in bed this morning too.

Exercise 14 Sam's Schedule.

Sam's Schedule

	A.M.	P.M.
MON	*Quick-Stop Mart* *Safeway*	*Ned's Sausage Shop* *Short-Stop at 24th St.*
TUE	*McDonald's*	*Mama Luisa's Italian Restaurant*
WED	*Wen-Po's Chinese Kitchen*	*The Burger Place* *The Springfield Country Club*
THU	*Western Round-up Steaks*	*Big Joe's Steak House* *Taylor College Cafeteria*
FRI	*Pete's Pizza Palace* *Safeway*	*Wash the truck*
SAT		
SUN		

Now answer the questions about Sam and his schedule for the week.

1. Where ___was___ Sam on Wednesday morning? ___At Wen-Po's Chinese Kitchen.___
2. When ________ Sam at McDonald's? ________________________
3. What ________ on Sam's schedule for Thursday morning? ________________________
4. Where ________ Sam on Monday afternoon? ________________________
5. When ________ Sam on 24th Street? ________________________
6. When ________ Sam at the Springfield Country Club? ________________________
7. What ________ on Sam's schedule Tuesday afternoon? ________________________
8. When ________ Sam at Pete's Pizza Palace? ________________________
9. When ________ Sam at the Taylor College cafeteria? ________________________
10. When ________ Sam at Safeway Supermarket? ________________________

Extra Credit: When ________ the truck clean? (Present tense or Past tense?)

____

Exercise 15 Where Were You Then?

Finish the sentences. Use the BE *verb and an adverb of place (single word or prepositional phrase).*

1. Where were you a minute ago? I ___was in the hall.___
2. Where were you an hour ago? I ________________________
3. Where were you two hours ago? I ________________________
4. Where were you yesterday? I ________________________
5. Where were you yesterday morning? I ________________________
6. Where were you two days ago? I ________________________
7. Where were you a week ago? I ________________________
8. Where were you a month ago? I ________________________

9. Where were you last year? I ______________________________

10. Where were you two years ago? I ______________________________

11. Where were you last week? I ______________________________

12. Where were you last Tuesday? I ______________________________

2.5 Compare Present and Past Tenses

Present Tense Words and Phrases:

now	*today*	*this morning*
this afternoon	*this evening*	*tonight*

Example Sentences in Context:

NOTE: In English the present tense can also have future meaning with a future time word.

I am busy **today.** (now and all day)

I have classes **today.** (later today)

This morning I have a class. (later this morning)

This afternoon I have a test.

I have a meeting **this evening. Tonight** I study with Pat.

Past Tense Words and Phrases:

then	*yesterday*	*yesterday morning*
yesterday afternoon	*yesterday evening*	*last hour*
last night	*last week*	*last month*
last year	*last spring*	*last fall*
last summer	*last winter*	*last Monday*
last April	*last New Year's Day*	*a year ago*

Example Sentences:

The children were busy **yesterday.**

They were sleepy **yesterday morning.**

They were at school **yesterday afternoon.**

They were in bed early **last night.**

They were quiet **then.**

Sue is here **now.**

Last summer she was in Europe.

Last fall she was in Asia.

Last winter she was in Brazil.

She was in Panama **last March.** That's almost **a year ago.**

She was in New York **last week,** but she is here **now.**

NOTE: "Yesterday but at night" = "last night." ("They were home last night.") English speakers don't say, "Yesterday night."

Exercise 16 Here is Amy's Time Schedule for Last Week.

	Monday	Tuesday	Wednesday	Thursday	Friday	Saturday
morning	class	class	dentist	class	library	baseball game
afternoon	class	meeting	class	lab	class	
evening	library	no class	library	class	party	dinner at Pat's

Use Amy's time schedule to complete the sentences. Here are some expressions to use:

at class/in class
at the lab/in the lab
on Monday
at the library
at a party
on Friday afternoon
at a meeting
at a baseball game
on Saturday morning
at the dentist's office
at Pat's for dinner
on Wednesday evening

1. Amy ________________ last Wednesday morning.
2. Last Saturday afternoon, ________________.
3. Amy ________________ last Friday night.
4. Amy ________________ last Wednesday afternoon.
5. When was Amy at the dentist's office? ________________
6. When was there a baseball game? ________________
7. When was the library open? ________________
8. What day was there no class? ________________
9. When was the meeting? ________________
10. When was Amy in the lab? ________________
11. When was Pat's dinner? ________________
12. When was Amy (probably) in bed, sleeping late? ________________

Exercise 17 Rain.

Change these sentences from present time to past time.

1. We need rain. The grass is brown and yellow. We needed rain.
2. The tree in the back yard is almost dead. ______
3. The forests are very dry. ______
4. The danger of fire is high. ______
5. The air is hot and dusty. ______
6. There are clouds in the sky. ______
7. There is some lightning and thunder. ______
8. There is rain in the air. ______

Exercise 18 Robert, the Bus Driver.

Robert takes students on special trips. This list is his schedule for last week.

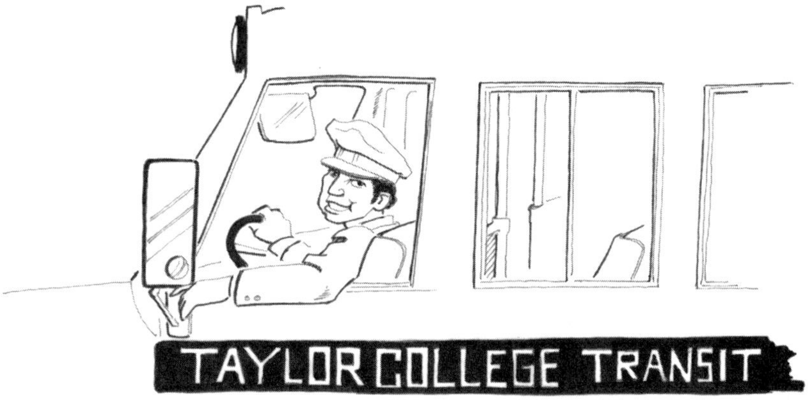

	Morning	Afternoon	Evening
Monday:	museum downtown	baseball park for game	the Little Theater
Tuesday:	geology class trip to Big Canyon	————————→	
Wednesday:	—	art museum	concert
Thursday:	zoo	volleyball tournament	————→
Friday:	Goodman Park for class picnic	————————→	

Now answer questions about Robert's schedule for last week. Use time adverbials like last Monday, *or* on Friday evening.

1. Robert was at Big Canyon ___on Tuesday___ .
2. He __________ at the zoo __________.
3. Robert __________ at the art museum __________.
4. He __________ at a concert __________.
5. When __________ Robert at Goodman Park? __________
6. Why __________ Robert there? __________
7. When __________ Robert downtown? __________
8. Why __________ Robert downtown? __________
9. When __________ Robert at a volleyball game? __________
10. Robert's bus is dirty. When __________ there time to wash it? __________

Review and Preview

Make a sentence like this:

Subject	+ VERB	+ REST OF SENTENCE
Noun Pronoun Name This/That Those/These	be has/have	adjective adverb of place (and time) noun pronoun absolute possessive

Make a yes/no question like this:

FIRST VERB + Subject + REST OF SENTENCE

NOTE: In a question with the verb BE, use only BE.

Sentence: He is a student here now.
Question: Is he a student here now?

Sentence: He has good grades in English class.
Question: Does he have good grades in English class?

Make a question-word question like this:

QUESTION WORD + BE + Subject
or QUESTION WORD + DO/DOES + Subject + REST OF SENTENCE

Sentence: Tom Turner is a good student.
Question: Who is a good student?

Sentence: Tom Turner is a good student.
Question: What is Tom Turner?

Sentence: Tom gets goods grades in math.
Question: What does Tom get in math?
Who gets good grades in math? (*Who* is the subject here.)

Numbers

1	one	1st	first	single
2	two	2nd	second	double or twice (twin)
3	three	3rd	third	three times (triple)
4	four	4th	fourth	four times (quadruple)
5	five	5th	fifth*	five times (quintuple)
6	six	6th	sixth	six times (sextuple)
7	seven	7th	seventh	seven times
8	eight	8th	eighth	eight times
9	nine	9th	ninth*	nine times
10	ten	10th	tenth	ten times
11	eleven	11th	eleventh	
12	twelve	12th	twelfth*	
13	thirteen	13th	thirteenth	
14	fourteen	14th	fourteenth	
15	fifteen	15th	fifteenth	
16	sixteen	16th	sixteenth	
17	seventeen	17th	seventeenth	
18	eighteen	18th	eighteenth	
19	nineteen	19th	nineteenth	
20	twenty	20th	twentieth*	
21	twenty-one	21st	twenty-first	
22	twenty-two	22nd	twenty-second	
23	twenty-three	23rd	twenty-third	
24	twenty-four	24th	twenty-fourth	
30	thirty	30th	thirtieth*	
40	forty	40th	fortieth*	
50	fifty	50th	fiftieth*	
60	sixty	60th	sixtieth*	
70	seventy	70th	seventieth*	
80	eighty	80th	eightieth*	
90	ninety	90th	ninetieth*	
100	one hundred	100th	one hundredth	
1000	one thousand	1000th	one thousandth	
10,000	ten thousand	10,000th	ten thousandth	
100,000	one hundred thousand	100,000th	one hundred thousandth	
1,000,000	one million	1,000,000th	one millionth	

*Be careful! These are different.

Unit 3: HAS and HAVE

WE HAVE A NICE TOWN.

3.1 HAS/HAVE

Example Sentences in Context:

This is the Smith family.
Their house is next to the Clark's house.
The Smiths and the Clarks are neighbors.

The Smiths have three children.
This is George Smith. He is the district manager of Maple Leaf Supermarkets. He has a good job. He has an old car too.

This is Emily Smith. She is a housewife. She has a baby at home. The Smith's children are Peggy, Jerry, and Ricky.

Peggy is a senior in high school. She has a job at McDonald's after school.

Jerry is in junior high school. He is a good ball player. His team has a good record.

Ricky is the baby. He is two years old. He has lots of toys.

Subject	HAS/HAVE	Nouns
Mr. Smith	has	a good job.
She	has	a baby at home.
They	have	three children.

Example Sentences in Context:

Hi! Pat.
We have a game today.
Are you ready?
Yes. Where is the ball?
I have the ball, a bat, and my shoes.
You have everything.
Let's go.

Subject	HAS/HAVE	Noun
I	have	the ball.
We	have	a game today.
You	have	everything.

Summary

I have the ball.
We have a game today.
You have everything.
He has a job.
She has a baby.
He has a new car.
It has a good motor.
They have a family.

Exercise 1 Let's Go Shopping!

Mrs. Smith and Peggy are at the store. Use has *or* have.

Mrs. Smith: Here's the shopping list. Let's buy some meat. They ________ chicken on sale.

Peggy: They ________ pizza on sale too.

Mrs. Smith: We ________ three pizzas at home in the freezer.

Peggy: Let's buy some hot dogs for the picnic.

Mrs. Smith: OK. They ________ some over there.

Peggy: Jerry ________ a game on Saturday. Let's buy some meat for sandwiches.

Exercise 2 With Peggy at McDonald's.

Use has/have *or* is/are.

Peggy ________ a job at McDonald's. It ________ a busy restaurant. She ________ there from four to seven. She ________ a job after school. McDonald's ________ a good worker. Peggy ________ a good student and a good worker.

Exercise 3 Mr. Smith's Model T.

Use has/have *or* is/are.

Mr. Smith ________ a hobby. He ________ an old car. It ________ a crank on the front. The seats ________ comfortable. They ________ soft. The dashboard ________ wood. The car ________ big. The car ________ a good motor. Mr. Smith ________ a special outfit. He ________ a special hat and gloves. He also ________ a long scarf and a long white coat.

Exercise 4 You Are a Lucky Man. Mini-Contexts.

Use has/have *or* am/is/are.

1.	Jerry	You ________ a great car, Dad.
	Mr. Smith:	Yes, I do. No, *we* do. We ________ lucky.
2.	Dr. Clark:	You ________ a lucky man, George.
		You ________ a nice family.
		You ________ a good job.
		And you ________ this car.
	Mr. Smith:	You ________ right. I ________ lucky, but you ________ too.
		You ________ a good job at Taylor College.
		You ________ a nice family too. And you ________ a new car.
3.	Peggy:	I ________ the car today. Let's go to the mall.
	Ann:	OK. I ________ some money. Let's buy some new clothes.
4.	Pam:	There ________ a big sale at the mall.
	Emily:	I know. Peggy ________ a new coat. It ________ blue. It ________ big buttons and a belt.
	Pam:	They ________ good sales at the mall. Ann ________ a new outfit too. It ________ a skirt and a sweater. It ________ gold buttons.

Exercise 5 Ann Clark.

Use has/have *to complete the sentences. Remember: use* HAVE *with* I, we, you, they. *Use* HAS *with* he, she, *and* it.

Ann Clark is a student at Taylor College. She ________ many friends. They all ________ a math class together. Ann ________ a job at the cafeteria, and her friends ________ part-time jobs too.

3.2 DO/DOES + Subject + HAS/HAVE {+ Noun?/+ Pronoun?}

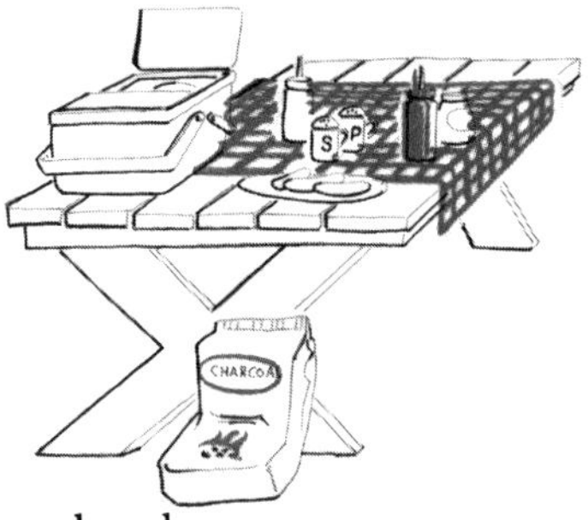

Example Sentences in Context:

Let's have a picnic!

Emily: I have some things for the picnic.
Pam: I do too. Do we have everything? I have some hot dogs.

Emily: Yes. Peggy put some things for the picnic in this box. She has the pickles and mustard.

Pam: Does she have any catsup there?

Emily: No, she doesn't. Do you have any?

Pam: Let me think. Do I have any? No, I don't.

Emily: Do you have any charcoal?

Pam: Yes, we do. We have one small bag. Does George have any?

Emily: Yes, he does. George has some in the garage.

DO/DOES	Subject	HAS/HAVE	Noun/Pronoun?	Answer
Do	I	have	any?	No, I don't.
Do	we	have	everything?	Yes, we do.
Do	you	have	the hot dog buns?	Yes, you do.
Does	she	have	catsup there?	No, she doesn't.
Does	he	have	any?	Yes, he does.
Do	they	have	catsup?	No, they don't.
Do	you?			Yes, I do.

Exercise 6 Let's Get Ready for Class!

Use do *with* have *to ask:* Do you have ________ ________ ________?

1. your books ____________________
2. a pen ____________________
3. a good pencil ____________________
4. some paper ____________________
5. your homework ____________________
6. a new notebook ____________________
7. a ruler ____________________
8. an eraser ____________________
9. some chalk ____________________
10. your backpack ____________________

Exercise 7 Where's My Notebook? Do You Have it? Mini-Contexts.

Use has *and* have *and* do, does, doesn't, don't.

1. Ann Where is my math notebook? ________ you ________ it?
   Bill: No, I ________. Let me look in the library.
   Ann: OK.
2. John: I have a big backpack. ________ you ________ one?
   Bob: Yes, I ________.
   John: Is it a strong one?
   Bob: Yes.
   John: Great! Let's take these books back to the library. You ________ a strong backpack, so you take these.
3. Peggy: Mom, let's do something tonight. Let's look in the newspaper. ________ we ________ a newspaper?
   Mrs. Smith: Yes, we ________. And today is Thursday. It's dollar-night at the movies. Let's go.
   Peggy: I ________ your car keys. Let's go now. It's almost seven o'clock.
   Mrs. Smith: OK.
4. Mrs. Smith: Hi, Pam. ________ you ________ a minute?
   Mrs. Clark: Sure, I ________. What's the matter?
   Mrs. Smith: It's the baby. He's sick. We ________ ________ any aspirin.
   Mrs. Clark: I ________ some. ________ he ________ a fever?
   Mrs. Smith: Yes, he ________.
5. George: How is your schedule this semester? ________ you ________ a good one?
   Ed: Yes, I'm lucky. I ________. I ________ only two large classes and a seminar.
   George: ________ you ________ a five-day schedule?
   Ed: Yes, unfortunately, I ________, but it's not too bad.
6. Jerry: Mom, I ________ a game tonight. ________ you ________ time to come?
   Emily: Well, maybe. ________ you ________ time to help me?
   Jerry: Sure.
   Emily: Let's wash the dishes, and then go!

Summary

Compare BE and HAVE

This is my book.	= I have a book.	(And this is it.)
That is our car.	= We have a car.	(And that is it.)
This is your pen.	= You have a pen.	(And this is it.)
This is her book.	= She has a book.	(And this is it.)
That is his backpack.	= He has a backpack.	(And that is it.)
That is their car.	= They have a car.	(And that is it.)

Exercise 8 All About Springfield.

Use BE *or* HAVE.

Springfield

Springfield __________ my hometown. It __________ a small city and a nice place to live. Springfield __________ a new mall at the south end of town. It __________ on Main Street.

The mall __________ many shops. Ruby's Department Store __________ there, and Martin's __________ too. The Clothes Line shop __________ clothes for the whole family. L & J's Men's Store __________ suits, shirts, and ties for men. They __________ the latest fashions for men and boys. The best women's store __________ the Hanger.

Springfield __________ a large hospital on the hill. The airport __________ on the highway at the north end of town. The new library __________ near the park. Springfield __________ a bus station. Springfield __________ a business section downtown. The drugstore, post office, some offices, and two restaurants __________ also downtown.

The high school __________ on Second Street. The middle school __________ two buildings on Third Street. The elementary school __________ near them on Third Street. Springfield also __________ a college, Taylor College.

The people of Springfield __________ three supermarkets. One of them __________ on the east side, and one __________ on the west side of town. The third one __________ in the middle.

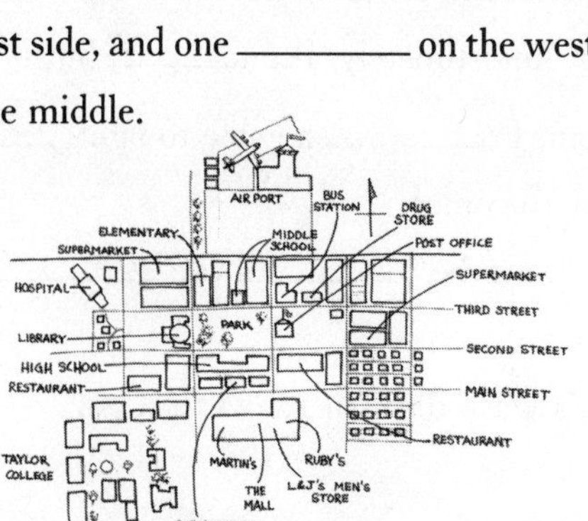

Exercise 9 Yes, I Do.

Use do/does *to complete the sentences. Remember: use* **DO** *with* I, we, you, they. *Use* **DOES** *with* he, she, it.

Ann and her parents are ready to go on a picnic.

Ann: ________ you have the charcoal, Dad?

Ed: Yes, I ________. ________ we have mustard?

Ann: Mom said yes, she ________.

Ed: ________ she have everything?

Ann: Yes, she ________.

3.3 Is THIS/THAT + Possessive Noun/Pronoun?

Example Sentences in Context:

Jim: I don't have my new pen. Where is it?

Ted: Well, whose is this pen? Is this yours? It was on the floor.

Jim: Yes, thanks. That's mine.

Summary

This is my book.	= I have a book.	= This book is mine.
That is our car.	= We have a car.	= That car is ours.
This is your pen.	= You have a pen.	= This pen is yours.
This is her book.	= She has a book.	= This book is hers.
That is his backpack.	= He has a backpack.	= That backpack is his.
That is their car.	= They have a car.	= That car is theirs.

Exercise 10 A New Family in Town.

Use my, our, your, his, her, their, *or* mine, ours, yours, his, hers, theirs.

The Walkers are a new family in town. ________ house is across the street from the Smith's house. This is Jason Walker. He is an executive at TTT Electronics. Mrs. Sara Walker is the new administrator of Springfield General Hospital. Jason and Sara have three children. ________ girls are twins, ________ names are Allison and Amy. ________ son Gary is in seventh grade.

The Hanson Brothers' moving van is here. Mr. and Mrs. Walker talk to Frank and Fred Hanson.

Frank:	Is this box for the kitchen?
Mr. Walker:	Yes, it is. Here's a bed, and it's not ___*mine*___. Is this ___*your*___ bed, Allison?
Allison:	Yes, it's ________, and that is ________ chair too.
Mr. Walker:	Here's a dresser, and it's not mine. Is that ________ dresser, too? This stuff is all ________, isn't it?
Allison:	No, it's Amy's. This box is ________ too.
Fred:	What is this bedroom furniture, Mr. Walker? Is it ________ and Mrs. Walker's?
Mr. Walker:	Yes, all the furniture over there is ________. And these chairs are ________ too.
Mrs. Walker:	Where is Gary's stuff?
Mr. Walker:	This box is ________, but where is ________ bed?

Summary

I ⟶ my house ⟶ mine
we ⟶ our house ⟶ ours
you ⟶ your house ⟶ yours
he ⟶ his house ⟶ his
she ⟶ her house ⟶ hers
they ⟶ their house ⟶ theirs

Exercise 11 Mrs. Walker's First Day at Work.

Use possessive pronouns to fill in the blanks.

Dr. Mark Fronski: Good morning, Mrs. Walker. I'm Mark Fronski, Chief of Staff. We have a fine hospital here. Welcome to Springfield General.

Mrs. Walker: Thank you, Dr. Fronski. It is nice of you to welcome me. And I'm glad to meet you.

Dr. Fronski: ________ hospital is large and modern. We have the best equipment and a fine staff. Let's walk around.

Mrs. Walker: Is this ________ office?

Dr. Fronski: No, this is Dr. Miller's office. He is the head of radiology. He always has ________ office near the emergency room and X-ray. ________ office is upstairs. (Mrs. Walker's)

Mrs. Walker: Where is ________ office? (Dr. Fronski's)

Dr. Fronski: ________ is near ________. (Your office is near my office.)

Mrs. Walker: Does Springfield General have a children's ward?

Dr. Fronski: Yes. The director is Dr. Shirley Cook. In fact, this office is ________.

Mrs. Walker: Is she here?

Dr. Fronski: Let's ask ________ secretary.

3.4 THERE + BE

Example Sentences in Context:

Mrs. Walker:	This is our new house. There is a large kitchen. There is a comfortable living room. Downstairs there is a garage for the cars. There's a dining room next to the kitchen. There are four bedrooms upstairs. There are also two bathrooms. There is also a big attic for boxes and suitcases.
Mrs. Smith:	There is?
Mrs. Walker:	Yes, there is.
Mrs. Smith:	Is there a basement?
Mrs. Walker:	No, there isn't.

THERE	BE	Adjective	Noun	Adverb
There	is	a large	kitchen.	
There	are	four	bedrooms	upstairs.
There	is?			

Exercise 12 Amy and Allison Talk About Their New House.

Use there is *or* there are.

Amy: This house is fantastic! ________ ________ four bedrooms, and they are all big.

Ally: ________ ________ two bathrooms too. ________ ________ two bathtubs!

Amy: ________ ________ a big closet in the bathroom too.

Ally: ________ ________? Where is it?

Amy: Behind the door. ________ ________ space for towels and blankets.

Ally: ________ ________ a big closet in each bedroom.

Amy: Yes, and ________ ________ space for boxes and suitcases in the attic.

Ally: ________ ________ a laundry room?

Amy: Yes, ________ ________. It's next to the kitchen.

Exercise 13 Jerry and Gary on a Bike Ride.

Use BE *verbs with* THERE *or pronouns (I, you, he, she) to complete the sentences.*

Jerry: Hi, I ________ Jerry Smith. My house ________ over there, across the street.

Gary: Hi!

Jerry:	You have a nice bike. Let's go for a ride.
Gary:	OK, let's go! _______ _______ a baseball field around here?
Jerry:	Sure! _______ _______ one at the corner of Grand and Second Avenue.
Gary:	Where _______ the movie theater? _______ _______ one in town?
Jerry:	Of course. _______ _______ three! _______ _______ one at the mall. _______ _______ another one downtown, and _______ _______ one at Taylor College.
Gary:	Where _______ the library?
Jerry:	It _______ near the park.
Gary:	What _______ up on the hill?
Jerry:	That _______ Springfield General Hospital!
Gary:	Oh! That _______ my mom's hospital. _______ _______ another hospital in town?
Jerry:	No, that _______ the only one.
Gary:	_______ _______ a supermarket near here?
Jerry:	Sure. _______ _______ one on Fourth and Main Street. _______ _______ two others, on the east and west.
Gary:	_______ _______ an ice cream shop?
Jerry:	Yes, _______ _______ one on Oak Street. I have some money. Let's go!

Exercise 14 Gary's Class.

Use there is *for a singular noun, and* these are *for a plural noun.*

Gary:	There _______ twenty-three kids in my class. There _______ twelve boys and eleven girls. There _______ only one teacher, Mrs. Garcia.
Sara:	Is she nice?
Gary:	Yes, but there _______ only one thing, Mom. She's strict!

3.5 THERE + BE (Past Tense)

Example Sentences in Context:

Springfield *was* a small town twenty-five years ago. There *were* only 8,000 people in Springfield then. There *was* one school.

Explanation:

There was one school. = Springfield had one school. (singular)

There were only 8,000 people in Springfield. = Springfield had only 8,000 people. (plural)

Exercise 15 Springfield Then and Now.

Use was *with a singular noun after* there, *and use* were *with a plural noun after* there.

Today Springfield is a small city of 20,000, but only twenty-five years ago ________ only 8,000 people. Then ________ no mall, but ________ a downtown shopping area. Twenty-five years ago, ________ only one small drugstore on First Avenue, and today ________ still ________. Then ________ no Country Club, but ________ a big farm there. Then ________ no supermarkets, only small grocery stores. ________ no airport, but ________ a bus station. ________ two restaurants, then, but ________ many today. Twenty-five years ago ________ no big businesses in town, but now ________ several. Now ________ an electronics company, TTT Electronics. ________ also a large flour mill. ________ a large bakery in Springfield too.

Exercise 16 How Was Your Day? Mini-Contexts.

Use there was, there were, was, *or* were.

1. Mr. W: How as your first day at work?

   Mrs. W: It was great. ________ several doctors at our meeting. They ________ glad to meet me, and I ________ glad to meet them.

   Mr. W: ________ any other administrators there?

   Mrs. W: Yes, ________. Everyone ________ there. We had a good meeting.

2. Ally: Hi, Peggy!

   Peggy: Hi! How was your first day at Springfield High?

   Ally: Fantastic. ________ so many new people, and they were all so friendly.

Peggy: ________ a big meeting for everyone in the school. You were there, weren't you?

Ally: Yes, I sure was.

3. Amy: How was your bike ride?

Gary: Fun! This is a great town. ________ some kids in the ball park. Last year ________ six baseball teams here.

Amy: Is Jerry a ball player too?

Gary: Yes, he is. ________ a team from this neighborhood.

4. Pamela: How was campus today?

Ann: Awful! ________ two thousand people there for a meeting. ________ no parking places in the parking lot. ________ hundreds of people in the cafeteria. ________ no place for a student to sit down.

5. George: ________ an accident on Fifth Avenue.

Emily: Oh?

George: ________ three cars and a big truck, off the road.

Emily: Was anyone hurt?

George: Yes, I think so. ________ a boy with a broken leg, ________ a women with a broken arm. And ________ two men with cuts and bruises.

6. Ed Clark has a Model T. ________ many cars like it in the 1920's and 1930's. ________ other cars too, but ________ none as popular as the Model T Ford.

Exercise 17 Springfield in Past Time.

Use was *for singular and* were *for plural nouns.*

Springfield today is different from twenty-five years ago. There ________ farms all around the town. There ________ no supermarkets. There ________ one drugstore, downtown. There ________ more trees and lots of empty lots. There ________ only one movie theater.

Unit 4: BE Verbs with Adjectives and Adverbs

IT WAS COOL THIS MORNING.

4.1 IT + BE + Adjective (+ Adverb)

Example Sentenccs in Context:

It is warm now, but it was cool this morning. It isn't cool now. It is sunny today, but it wasn't yesterday. It was cloudy and rainy.

Exercise 1 Seasons in Springfield.

Use it is *or* it was *to talk about the weather.*

Springfield has four seasons. In April ________ often rainy. In May ________ usually sunny and warm. In June ________ always warm. In July and August ________ never cold. ________ always hot in the summer. September begins fall. In September ________ cool at night and chilly in the mornings. By noon ________ usually warm. The snow comes in November, and ________ cold sometimes. In the winter months of December, January, and February, ________ often cold and snowy. Sometimes there is ice on the road, and ________ foggy. The roads are dangerous then. In March ________ windy.

Last winter ________ very cold. In December ________ snowy. Sometimes ________ icy too. In March ________ very windy, but in April ________ warm and rainy. Last summer ________ hot.

Summer

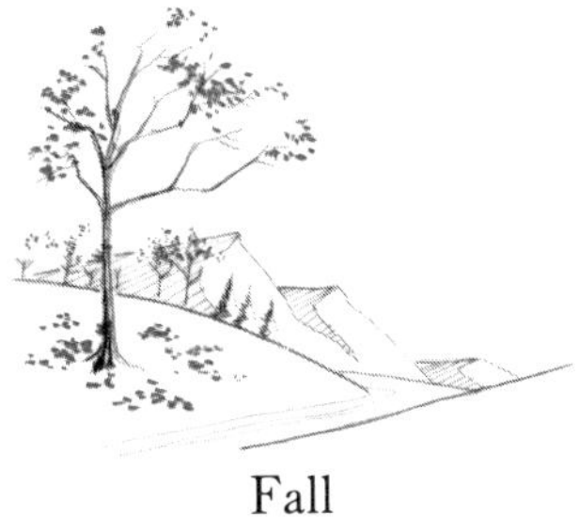
Fall

Winter

Spring

IT	BE	Verb + *-ing*
It	is	raining.
It	was	snowing.
It	is	hailing.

IT	BE	Adjective
It	was	icy.
It	is	snowy.
It	was	warm.

Exercise 2 Talk About the Weather.

Use it *to talk about weather:* It is + Adjective *or* It is + Verb *with* -ing.

1. Weather Reporter: This is Dawn Watson for WSPR-TV. Today in Springfield, it ________ warm and sunny. It ________ rain________ on the west coast and cool.

2. Weather Reporter: It ________ snow________ in Chicago today. The temperature ________ 30 degrees Fahrenheit, and the wind ________ blow________ in from Lake Michigan at about 25 miles an hour.

3. Weather Reporter: Today in Toronto, it ________ sunny and warm. It ________ warm and humid.

4. Weather Reporter: Here is the weather report for the Northern Hemisphere. In Mexico City, it ________ hot and dry today. It ________ rain________ in Acapulco, and it ________ cool in Sonora. In the US, it ________ cloudy in the West, and it ________ warm and sunny on the East Coast. It ________ rain________ in the Rocky Mountains. In Vancouver, it ________ cloudy and rain________. In the Canadian Rockies, it ________ snow________. In Montreal, it ________ a beautiful day. It ________ partly cloudy.

5. Weather Reporter: It ________ sunny today in Hawaii, but it ________ muggy and humid in Guam.

6. Weather Reporter: In Alaska today, it ________ rain________ and hail________.

Exercise 3 Weather Words.

Use these words to do the exercise.

cold	sunny	dry	snowing	stormy
chilly	partly cloudy	humid	sleeting	windy
cool	cloudy	muggy	hailing	breezy
pleasant	gloomy		raining	calm
nice	foggy			
warm	rainy			
hot				

Note to Teacher: Point out to the students that these words are arranged along a scale. The top word is one extreme of the scale, and the last word is the other extreme.

1. Today it is ________________.
2. Yesterday it was ________________.
3. In September it was ________________.
4. On my birthday it was ________________.
5. Now it is ________________.

Exercise 4 Talk About the Weather Today and Yesterday.

Use it is *or* it was *and a word or words from the chart to complete these sentences. Use* but *between the two ideas.*

Example: Today *it is* warm, *but* yesterday *it was* cool.

1. (cloudy, sunny) ______________________________
2. (stormy, calm) ______________________________
3. (snowing, raining) ______________________________
4. (windy, breezy) ______________________________
5. (breezy, calm) ______________________________
6. (gloomy, sunny) ______________________________
7. (sunny, foggy) ______________________________
8. (warm, hot) ______________________________
9. (humid, muggy) ______________________________
10. (cool, nice) ______________________________
11. (pleasant, chilly) ______________________________
12. (snowing, sleeting) ______________________________

Exercise 5 Joe's Steakhouse.

Use IT + BE + *Adjective.*

Jason: How's the food at Joe's Steakhouse?

Ed: ________ good!

Jason: The steak?

Ed: ________ great! ________ tender and juicy.

Jason: ________ expensive?

Ed: ________ not cheap, but ________ reasonable.

Use and *to join similar things.*

Two nouns:	Dave and Mark salt and pepper
Two verbs:	stop and listen watch and wait
Two sentences:	I am a student, and I have a class now. You have my keys, and I have yours.

Use but *to join opposite ideas.*

He *is poor but happy.*

He is poor, but he is happy.

Exercise 6 This and That, But Not That. Mini-Contexts.

Use and *or* but *to join the ideas in these sentences.*

1. Peggy is a student in high school. She has lots of friends, ________ she doesn't have much free time. She has a job at McDonald's, ________ she works twenty hours a week.
2. Mr. Smith is the district manager of Maple Leaf Supermarkets, ________ he likes his job. He is a hard worker, ________ he gets a month of vacation each year. He has a family, ________ he likes to be with them.
3. Ann Clark is a student at Taylor College, ________ so is Bill Henderson. They are friends, ________ they are in many classes together. Ann has Math 100, ________ Bill does too. Ann has a geology class, ________ Bill has physics at that time. Ann has a job at the cafeteria, ________ Bill doesn't work on campus. He has a job at Radio Hut, ________ he doesn't like it. He likes the people ________ the money, ________ he doesn't like the hours.
4. Amy ________ Ally are twins. They both have short hair, ________ they have beautiful eyes. Amy is tall, ________ so is Ally. Amy has a boyfriend, ________ Ally doesn't. Ally is a tennis player, ________ Amy isn't. Amy is friendly, ________ Ally is friendly too.

5. Emily Smith doesn't have a job outside her home, ________ she works very hard. She has three children, ________ one of them is a baby. His name is Ricky, ________ he is a healthy, happy baby. Emily's daughter is Peggy, ________ Emily is proud of her. Peggy is an honor student, ________ she works to save money for college. Emily's other son is Jerry. Jerry likes baseball, ________ he doesn't like to play football.

6. Ed Clark is a family man. He has a wife ________ a daughter. He is a teacher ________ a writer. He teaches English at Taylor College, ________ writes short stories for magazines. Ed is always busy, ________ he is always home after school. He likes to play golf with his wife, ________ he often goes fishing with his family.

Exercise 7 Good But Not Good Enough.

Use but *to join sentences with contrary outcomes (not what you expect).*

Examples: Ann: This is hot.
Amy: Yes, but not hot enough.

Ann: That coat isn't expensive.
Pam: That's true, but we still can't buy it.

Jane: Let's go to Pete's for pizza.

Kate: That's OK, ________ I'm on a diet.

Jane: Let's go to McDonald's for hamburgers.

Kate: OK, ________ it's too far, and I don't have much time.

Jane: Let's go to Wen-Po's.

Kate: OK, I like Chinese food, ________ it's not expensive.

4.3 Adverbs of Frequency with BE + HAVE

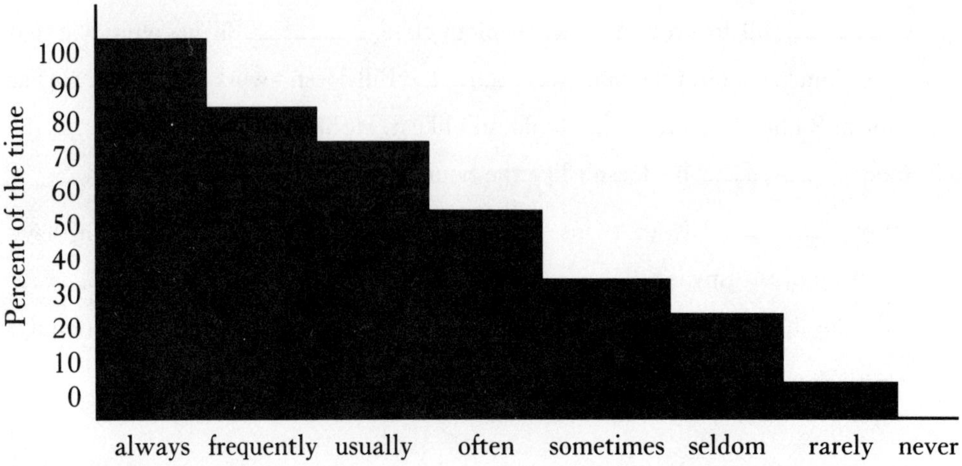

Example Sentences in Context:

I am *always* on time.
I'm *frequently* here an hour before class.
I am *usually* here before you.
I am *often* the first one here.
Ann, you are *sometimes* late.
Tom is *seldom* here on time.
Kate is *rarely* late.
She's *never* absent.

NOTE: These sentences use *BE*. The adverb of frequency comes after the BE verb.

I *always* have breakfast at seven o'clock.
I *frequently* have two cups of coffee.
I *never* have tea, but my mother *always* does.

NOTE: In sentences with *have* (and *do/does*), the adverb of frequency comes before the verb.

Exercise 8 Sam's Schedule.

Write these sentences about Sam.

1. Sam is a truck driver. He is at work by 8:00. (always) ______________________
2. He has breakfast before 7:00. (usually) ______________________
3. On Mondays, he is at Ned's Sausage Shop in the afternoon. (always) ______________________
4. He has a clean truck on Thursdays. (never) ______________________
5. He has lunch at Pete's Pizza Palace on Fridays. (usually) ______________________
6. He has a coffee break at 10:30. (often) ______________________
7. Sam is early on Fridays. (frequently) ______________________
8. On Fridays he leaves early. (sometimes) ______________________

9. He is at home before six. (seldom) ______________________

____

10. Sam is absent from work. (rarely) ______________________

____

Exercise 9 What Is True About You?

Add adverbs from the list (always . . . never).

1. I have breakfast. ______________________
2. I am on time for class. ______________________
3. I have classes in the morning. ______________________
4. I am ready for my classes. ______________________
5. I have lunch in the cafeteria. ______________________
6. I go to the movies. ______________________
7. I go swimming. ______________________
8. I go to the library to study. ______________________
9. I am friendly. ______________________
10. I am tired at night. ______________________

Exercise 10 What Do You Do?

Ask a friend these questions. Then write about your friend. Use adverbs of frequency.

1. Do you have breakfast? ______________________

____

2. Are you on time for class? ______________________

____

3. Do you have classes in the morning? ______________________

____

4. Are you ready for your classes? ______________________

____

5. Do you have lunch in the cafeteria? ______________________

____

6. Do you go to the movies? ______________________

____

7. Do you go swimming? ______________________

____

8. Do you go to the library to study? ______

9. Are you friendly? ______

10. Are you tired at night? ______

Exercise 11 Sometimes.

Add adverbs of frequency (after BE *verbs, but before* HAS *and* HAVE*). Write these sentences again with the adverbs of frequency in the right place.*

(always) Dr. Hunter has a new math class in the fall.

______

(usually) He has more than thirty students.

______

(often) There are more than forty students in his class.

______

(frequently) His students have homework.

______

(sometimes) They have quizzes.

______

(seldom) There is a midterm exam.

______

(rarely) Dr. Hunter is absent from class.

______

(never) There is a term paper in his class.

______

4.4 Commands, Requests, and Suggestions

Example Sentences in Context:

Ed: I have an appointment with the doctor at 9.
Pam: You're late. It's almost nine o'clock now.
Ed: Oh, no! Please help me!
Call the doctor's office.
Tell them that I'm coming.
Then find my car keys!
And where's my coat?
Pam: Here it is. Now please drive carefully.

Adverb	(Please)	Verb	Rest of Sentence
	Please	help	me!
		Call	the doctor's office.
		Tell	them that I'm coming.
Then		find	my car keys!
Now	please	drive	carefully.

Grammar Note: All of these commands, requests, and suggestions use the simple verb. There is no subject necessary. *Please help me!* means *You help me* or *I need your help. Now please drive carefully* means *Please (I ask you) you (to) drive carefully now.*

Exercise 12 Help Me! Mini-Contexts.

Fill in the blank with a command or request. Here are some words to use:

ask	call	check out	do	drive	fill
find	give	go	help	look around	look at
open	pour	press	push	put	read
ride	sweep	take (it) out	take it back	tell	turn (it) on
turn (it) off	walk	wash	wipe		

1. Jerry: Where is my backpack?
   Mother: It's on the shelf.
   Jerry: It's too high for me. ________________ ________________
   Mother: OK. Here it is.
2. Ed: There was just a car accident on the corner! ________________ the police.
   Pam: Is anyone hurt?
   Ed: I think so. ________________ an ambulance.
3. Gary: I'm bored.
   Amy: ________________ TV.
   Gary: I'm bored with TV.
   Amy: ________________ your homework.
   Gary: My homework is finished.
   Amy: ________________ your bike.
   Gary: Well . . . , maybe.
   Amy: OK, then ________________ Jerry. ________________ on a bike ride with him.

Gary: That's a good idea.

4. Pam: Here are the groceries. ________________ me, Ed.

Ed: OK. ________________ me what to do.

Pam: ________________ the cans on the shelf.

________________ the meat in the refrigerator.

________________ the fruit in the fruit bowl.

5. Ally: This is a hard job. ________________ me, Mom.

Sara: OK, honey. Let me help you. First ________________ me the pieces. Then, ________________ me the glue. Next, ________________ together these big pieces.

Ally: OK, Mom, I can do it. Thanks.

6. (Andy is a new worker at McDonald's.)

Peggy: Andy, let me help you. Let's work together.

Andy: OK. ________________ me learn the job.

Peggy: In the morning ________________ on the grill for the eggs and hamburgers. Then ________________ out some food from the freezer. The food is in bags. So ________________ one bag of each kind.

Andy: Is this the milk shake machine?

Peggy: Yes. That's the next lesson. ________________ the milk shake mix. It is in this carton. ________________ it into the top. ________________ the machine early in the morning. We have three kinds of milk shakes: vanilla, chocolate, and strawberry. ________________ the vanilla button on the machine for a vanilla milk shake.

7. (It's 10 p.m. at McDonald's.)

Peggy: It's clean-up time, Andy. First, ________________ away all the food. Then ________________ off the grill. Next, ________________ all the tables and counters. Then ________________ the floor.

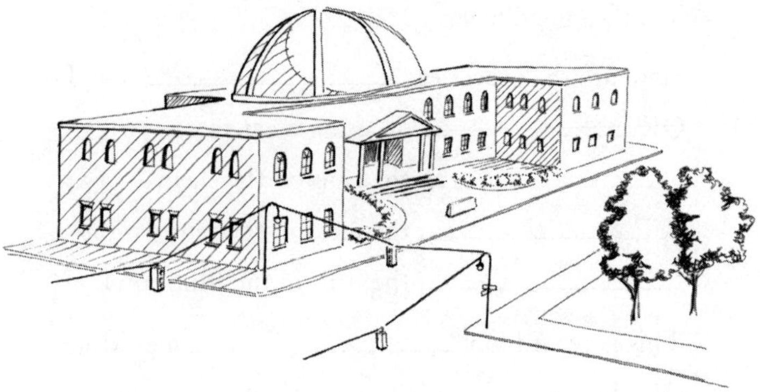

8. Learn about the library. (Use these words: *ask* (for), *check* (out), *fill* (out), *find, give, go, look* (around), *look* (at), *pick, read, take.*)

 ________________ to the library at the corner of Main and First Avenue.

 ________________ for a library card.

 ________________ out the application form.

 ________________ around the library.

 ________________ at the shelves.

 ________________ an interesting book.

 ________________ to the check-out counter.

 ________________ it to the librarian.

 ________________ out the book.

 ________________ it home and ________________ it.

 After two weeks ________________ it back to the library.

Exercise 13 It's Cold in Here.

Write a suggestion for each complaint.

1. It's cold in here. ________________
2. Now I'm hot. ________________
3. I'm bored. ________________
4. The door isn't open. ________________
5. The baby is hungry. ________________
6. There is nothing to eat in the refrigerator. ________________
 ____
7. I have no money. ________________
8. It's time for my favorite TV program. ________________
 ____

4.5 Commands, Requests, and Suggestions with *Not*

Example Sentences in Context:

Please come in.
But don't step on the rug.
First, please use the door mat.
Don't come into the house with dirty shoes.
Please sit down, but never sit over there.
That's Dad's chair.

Conjunction or Adverb	(Please)	(Don't)	Verb	Rest of Sentence
	Please		come	in.
But		don't	step	on the rug.
Never			sit	over there.
		Don't	come	into the house with dirty shoes.

Grammar Note: *Don't do that!* sometimes means *Never do that! Never* is a strong way to give negative command. It means *not ever,* so do not use *never* with *not.*

Exercise 14 School Rules.

Add don't *in appropriate places. Put a* ----- (dash) *if* don't *isn't necessary.*

At a high school there are lots of rules. Always ________ do your homework. ________ take your books to class. ________ be late; always ________ be on time. ________ talk to your teachers rudely; always ________ be polite. ________ run in the halls. ________ yell to your friends. Never ________ throw papers on the floor. ________ keep food in your locker. ________ write on anything but paper. ________ be a good citizen.

Exercise 15 Do This! Don't Do That! Mini-Contexts.

Use these verbs to complete the sentences. Add don't *where necessary.*

be	come	eat	forget	get
go	let	miss	open	put
remember	skip	take	talk	throw
wash	wear	write	yell	

1. Ed: Let's pay the bills. Here they are. ________________ out your checkbook.

   Pam: Here it is. I am ready.

   Ed: ________________ a check for $35.48 to the gas company. ________________ to write down our account number.

   Pam: ________________ so fast. What is our account number? (Use *don't.*)

   Ed: It's 333-459-6677. ________________ write it there! No, ________________ it here!

   Pam: Ed, you do it. I don't want to.

   Ed: I'm sorry. ________________ the number anywhere.

2. (In the kitchen)

   Gary: Hi, Mom. I'm hungry. Is there something to eat?

   Sara: Sure, but ________________ too long. ________________ your homework.

   Gary: OK. There are some hot dogs here.

   Sara: Please ________________ that package of hot dogs. They are for the picnic tomorrow.

   Gary: OK. Here are some potato chips.

   Sara: ________________ those! They are bad for your skin.

   Gary: Oh, well. There's a piece of pie.

   Sara: Oh, Gary, I'm sorry. That's your dad's. Please ________________ that. There are some pieces of fruit in the bowl. And some vegetables here too.

   Gary: Maybe later, Mom. With yogurt and spinach.

3. Jerry and Gary are at the baseball field. Their coach has a list of rules.

   Coach O'Brien: Hi, boys. Welcome back, Tigers! Let's go over the team rules:

   First: Never ________________ practice. ________________ on time every day.

   Second: ________________ to wear your uniform for our games. (Use *don't.*)

   Third: ________________ at the other team. Tigers are "good sports." (Use *don't.*)

   Fourth: Never ________________ the bat. That is dangerous.

   Fifth: Never ________________ the ball at another player. That is dangerous too.

NOTE: You throw a ball ***to*** a person, and he or she catches it. You throw a ball ***at*** a person, and it hurts him or her.

4. Let's get ready for a picnic.

Peggy: Where's the picnic basket?

Emily: In the garage. George, please ________________ it. And ________________ ________________ the charcoal.

Peggy: And Mom, please ________________ ________________ the mustard and catsup.

Emily: Right! And Peggy, ________________ your father for some help.

Unit 5: Present Time, Continuous Aspect

WHAT ARE THEY DOING NOW?

5.1 Present Time, Continuous Aspect

Subject	+	BE	+	Verb	+	-ing	(+Noun Object)	(Sentence)
Question Word	+	BE	+	Verb	+	-ing	(+Noun Object)	(Question)

Example Sentences in Context:

Emily: Peggy! What *are* you *doing* now?
Peggy: I*'m doing* my homework.
Emily: *Are* you *studying* math?
Peggy: No, I*'m reading* history.
Emily: I need help in the kitchen.
Peggy: Oh, Mom! What*'s* Jerry *doing*?
Emily: He *is helping* your father. They *are fixing* the car now.
Peggy: Jerry*'s* always *doing* something.
Emily: Peggy!
Peggy: I *am coming.*

Subject	BE	Verb + -ING	Object Noun
I	am	coming.	
I	'm	coming!	
I	am	doing	my homework.
We	are	working.	
You	are	studying	math.
He	is	helping	your father.
She	is	reading.	
They	are	fixing	the car.

BE	Subject	Verb + -ING	Object Noun
Are	you	studying	math?

Question Word	BE	Subject	Verb + -ING
What	are	you	doing?
What	is	Jerry	doing?
Where	is	Jerry	going?
How	is	Jerry	fixing the car?
When	is	Jerry	going to bed?
Why	is	Peggy	studying now?

Exercise 1 Learning to Drive.

Add is *or* are *and* -ing *to complete the sentences.*

Amy and Ally ___*are learning*___ to drive.
Jason ___*is teaching*___ them.

Jason: Amy! You ________ go________ too fast.

Amy: Dad, you ________ worry________ too much.

Jason: No, I ________ think________ about the police officer behind us.

Amy: Oh, no! ________ I speed________?

Jason: I hope not. Let's stop now. It's Ally's turn.

Ally: Where ________ we go________, Dad?

Jason: Let's go to Country Club Road.

Ally: OK. How ________ I do________, Dad?

Jason: Fine, just fine. You ________n't go________ too fast, and you ________n't talk________ too much. You ________ do________ just fine.

Exercise 2 Calling the Doctor.

Add is, are, *and* -ing. *Use an* X *to show a blank. (Nothing goes in a blank. No word is necessary.)*

NOTE: Only verbs need an *-ing.* Adjectives do not take *-ing.*

Example: Ricky ___is___ cough___ing___ a lot. He is sick___X___.

Emily ________ call________ the doctor's office. She wants to see the doctor. Now she ________ go________ to the doctor with Ricky. She ________ worry________ about him. He has a fever. He ________ never sick________.

Doctor: What ________ wrong________ with Ricky?

Emily: He ________ cough________ and cry________ a lot.

Doctor: ________ he sleep________ normally?

Emily: No, He ________n't. He ________ not sleep________, and neither am I.

Doctor: Let's take his temperature. When did he get sick?

Emily: Two days ago. He ________n't eat________, and he ________ fussy________.

Doctor: It ________ a cold, just a cold.

Exercise 3 Emily Goes Shopping.

Use the BE *verb and a verb with* -ing *to complete the paragraph.*

Emily ________ shop________ at the supermarket. She ________ buy________ the food for the week. She ________ check________ the prices carefully. Her family ________ also look________ around. They ________ find________ things to buy.

5.2 Changing Verbs to Verbs + *-ing*

Some Verbs Take just *-ing*:

go + *ing* ⟶ going
talk + *ing* ⟶ talking
dry + *ing* ⟶ drying

Verbs with Silent *e*, Drop the *e*:

giv*e* + ing ⟶ giving
driv*e* + ing ⟶ driving
hav*e* + ing ⟶ having

The *e* on Some Verbs Is "Real":

se*e* + ing ⟶ seeing
b*e* + ing ⟶ being

Some Verbs Double the Final Letter:

ge*t* + ing ⟶ getting
pu*t* + ing ⟶ putting
ho*p* + ing ⟶ hopping

How Do You Spell These Verbs with *-ing*?

1.	walk	__________	16.	listen	__________
2.	make	__________	17.	play	__________
3.	rest	__________	18.	agree	__________
4.	do	__________	19.	help	__________
5.	use	__________	20.	write	__________
6.	read	__________	21.	step	__________
7.	study	__________	22.	sit	__________
8.	rain	__________	23.	let	__________
9.	speak	__________	24.	stop	__________
10.	come	__________	25.	skip	__________
11.	say	__________	26.	free	__________
12.	wash	__________	27.	shave	__________
13.	fix	__________	28.	smoke	__________
14.	eat	__________	29.	swim	__________
15.	learn	__________	30.	fly	__________

NOTE: The present continuous means now or future, with adverbs.

Exercise 4 What Are You Doing? Mini-Contexts.

Complete the sentences using BE + VERB + -ing *change the spelling if necessary.*

1. Joe: What ________ you do________, Jane?
   Jane: I ________ read________ my history book.
   Joe: ________ you learn________ anything?
   Jane: Not really, I ________ review________ for a test.
2. Bill: Where ________ you go________, Mark?
   Mark: To the basketball court. Why?
   Bill: I ________ need________ some help with the math assignment. I ________ have________ trouble with algebra.
   Mark: It ________n't go________ well?

3. Ann: When ________ you leave________ for New York, Joe?
   Joe: I'________ leave________ at ten o'clock in the morning.
   Ann: ________ you stay________ there long?
   Joe: For two weeks. I'________ visit________ some relatives there.
4. Sara: It's time for bed, Gary!
   Gary: Yes, Mom. I know. I ________ wash________ my face.
   Sara: ________ you do________ a good job?
   Gary: Sure.
   Sara: And now, ________ you brush________ your teeth?
   Gary: Yes, Mom. I'________ do________ it.
   Sara: And now?
   Gary: I'________ get________ into bed now.
   Sara: Good night, son.
5. Pamela: Ed, look! A new family ________ move________ into the house on the corner.
   Ed: Oh? What ________ happen________?
   Pamela: Some people ________ unload________ a truck.
   Ed: And they ________ have________ trouble. Let's help.
6. Gloria: ________ everyone help________?
   Tony: Let me help. Oh, someone ________ come________ here from across the street.
   Ed: Do you need some help?
   Tony: We ________ try________ to get this table out of the truck.
   Ed: OK, let's go!

NOTE: The present continuous tense with adverbs of frequency sometimes means "The person is doing it *and* is not happy about it."

Exercise 5 What Are You Doing Now? Mini-Contexts.

Complete these sentences with BE *verbs and either verbs* +-ing *or adjectives. Rewrite the sentences.*

1. (watch) I ________________ TV now.
   (think) I ________________ not ________________ about anything important.

(rest) I ________ just ________.

(lazy) ________ I ________? My mother thinks so.

2. (busy) I ________ a ________ woman.

(do housework) I ________ always ________.

(clean) I ________ always ________ the house.

(cook) Or else I ________ breakfast, lunch, or dinner.

3. (bore) A student's life ________.

(study) Everyday we ________ something.

(write) Each week we ________ papers.

(take) At the end of every semester, we ________ exams.

4. (practice) Jerry is on the baseball team, so he ________ always ________.

(throw) Now he ________ the ball to his dad.

(make) He ________ his arm strong.

5. (work) Pam ________ out at the gym.

(exercise) Today she ________ in an aerobics class.

(run) She ________ around the track.

(swim) She ________ also ________ in the warm pool.

6. (golf) Ed ________ with his wife.

(hit) He ________ the ball well today,

(look) but now he ________ for his ball in the woods.

Exercise 6 Bill at the Gym.

Change the simple verbs to verbs with -ing. *(Change spelling)*

Bill ________ work________ out at the gym. He ________ lift________ weights and ride________ the exercise bicycle. He ________ stretch________ his muscles. He arms ________ get________ stronger. He ________ lose________ weight.

Dr. Hunter: Are you enjoying math class?
Joe: *Yes, I am.* Am I passing?
Dr. Hunter: Of course you are. Aren't the students finding it easy?
Joe: *No, they aren't.* It's too hard.
Dr. Hunter: Oh, really? Is your brother taking math too?
Joe: *Yes, he is.* He's taking Dr. Brown's class at 2:00. He's having an easier time.
Dr. Hunter: Ask him to help you.

Yes/No	Subject	BE
Yes,	I	am.
No,	we	aren't.
Yes,	you	are.
No,	you	aren't.
Yes,	he	is.
No,	she	isn't.
Yes,	they	are.

Answer yes *or* no. *Use the picture to check the information.*

1. Is the teacher reading a book? ________
2. Is Mary erasing the board? ________
3. Is Tommy closing the window? ________
4. Is Julie looking out the window? ________
5. Is Rachel reading? ________

6. Is Joshua tying his shoe? ________
7. Is the teacher talking? ________
8. Is Judy raising her hand? ________
9. Is Stacey writing in her notebook? ________
10. Are Rachel and Jan listening? ________
11. Are Todd and Billy drawing pictures? ________
12. Is Billy erasing the chalkboard? ________
13. Is Tommy tying his shoe? ________
14. Is Joshua closing the window? ________
15. Is Judy looking at a map? ________
16. Is Julie looking at the map? ________
17. Is Todd reading his social studies book? ________
18. Is Mary walking in? ________
19. Is Bart erasing the board? ________
20. Is Stacey walking in? ________

Exercise 7 Who is ______? She is.

Example: Who is talking? The teacher is. Rachel is.

1. Who is erasing the chalkboard? ______________
2. Who is reading? ______________
3. Who is tying his shoe? ______________
4. Who is looking at the map? ______________
5. Who is walking in late? ______________
6. Who is talking to the class? ______________
7. Which students are not listening? ______________
8. Who is closing the window? ______________
9. Who is writing in her notebook? ______________
10. Who is drawing a picture? ______________
11. Who is raising her hand? ______________
12. Who is talking with a friend? ______________

Exercise 8 Bart is Sitting.

Give short answers to present continuous questions.

Bart is in a big chair. He is reading a book, chewing gum, and drinking a soda.

Is he sitting on the couch? ________________

Is he reading a book? ________________

Is he chewing tobacco? ________________

Is he reading a newspaper? ________________

Is he drinking a soda? ________________

Is he sitting in a big chair? ________________

5.4 Verbs Like BE *(SEEM, TASTE, SMELL, FEEL, LOOK, SOUND)*

BE and these other verbs can take adjectives *after* the verb. In this way, they are like the BE verb. They have a continuing meaning, but these verbs do not often take an *-ing*. Another name for these verbs is verbs of the senses.

Example Sentences in Context:

Pam: This dress *feels* comfortable.
Ann: It *looks* good too.
Pam: Does it *seem* too dressy?
Ann: No, it doesn't. I don't think so.
Pam: OK. Let's buy it. And let's have lunch.
Ann: That *sounds* good. There is a pizza place here at the mall.
Pam: I know! I smell pizza, and it *smells* great.
Ann: It *tastes* good too. My friends and I always come here.

Summary

It feels comfortable.	⟶	It is comfortable.
It looks good.	⟶	It is good. (in appearance)
It seems dressy.	⟶	(Maybe) It is dressy.
That sounds good.	⟶	It is good. (in its sound)
It smells great.	⟶	It is great. (in the way it smells)
It tastes good too.	⟶	It is good. (to the taste)

NOTE: Here is the question form and the short answer.

Does it *seem* too dressy? No, it doesn't.

Notice the changes from DO to DOES and DON'T to DOESN'T.

I don't feel comfortable.	He doesn't feel comfortable.
We don't feel comfortable.	She doesn't feel comfortable.
You don't feel comfortable.	It doesn't feel comfortable.
They don't feel comfortable.	

Exercise 9 That Sounds Good to Me. Mini-Contexts.

Use one of the verbs like BE (feel, look, seem, sound, smell, taste) *to complete these contexts.*

1. Peggy: Hi, Ann, why are you here at the mall?
   Ann: There is a sale at Wilson's Shoe Store.
   Peggy: Hey! Let's go there together.
   Ann: That ________ good to me.
   Peggy: How do these shoes ________?
   Ann: They ________ fine, but how do they ________?
   Peggy: They ________ comfortable, and the price ________ reasonable.
2. Jerry: The chocolate ________ good.
   Gary: Look at that blueberry! I bet that ________ good.
   Jerry: Let's try it!
   Gary: Two blueberry ice cream cones, please.
   Jerry: Boy! Does this ________ good!
3. Sara: Supper's ready. Let's eat.
   Amy: What's for supper, Mom? It sure ________ good.
   Sara: It's roast chicken and baked potatoes.

Ally: Chicken? That ________ delicious.

Jason: It ________ really beautiful too. Thank you, Sara.

4. Pam: What's wrong with Ann?

Ed: I don't know. She ________ tired today.

Pam: Her face ________ pale. Oh, here she is . . . Ann, how do you ________?

Ann: Oh, I ________ a little weak and tired.

Ed: Why don't you go back to bed?

Ann: OK.

5. Amy: Well, Gary, today's your first ball game. You ________ good in your new baseball uniform.

Gary: Thanks, I am glad to have you all here for my first game.

Jason: It's great to be here.

Sara: The coach is calling you. He ________ eager to start.

Gary: Oh! See you later. . . .

Ally: The boys ________ handsome in their new uniforms.

Amy: Oh! Those hot dogs ________ good. Let's buy some! . . .

Sara: These hot dogs ________ delicious.

Jason: Look, they are selling popcorn. It ________ delicious. Do you want some?

Sara: No, let's not get popcorn. Let's not spoil our supper.

Amy: Mom, I ________ sick. I don't ________ good.

Exercise 10 At the Supermarket.

Use the verbs in parentheses to complete the sentences.

Mrs. Walker is at the supermarket with Gary.

Gary:	Mom, what is this green thing? It ________ bumpy. (feel) And it ________ funny, like a pear. (look)
Mrs. Walker:	That's an avocado. And it ________ ripe. (seem)
Gary:	What does an avocado taste like?
Mrs. Walker:	It ________ smooth and creamy. (taste) And it ________ fresh. (seem) Do you want to try one?
Gary:	Sure, Mom. That ________ good. (sound)

5.5 Negative Statements and Questions with Verbs like BE, SEEM, TASTE, SMELL, FEEL, LOOK, and SOUND.

Example Sentences in Context:

Sara:	That melon *doesn't seem* ripe, but this one *does.*
Gary:	That melon *doesn't smell* ripe, but this one *does.*
Sara:	That melon *doesn't feel* ripe, but this one *does.*
Gary:	That melon *doesn't look* ripe, but this one *does.*
Sara:	You still *don't seem* sure, so tap it! *Does* it *sound* ripe?
Gary:	Yes. And . . . um-m-m . . . it tastes *ripe,* too.
Sara:	Oh, *does* it? . . . um-m-m . . . Yes, it *does.*

Exercise 11 How Does It Look? Mini-Contexts.

Use the negative form of the verb in parentheses to complete the sentence.

1. (at Wilson's Shoes)

Jerry: These shoes ________ right. (feel)
Emily: They ________ big enough. (look)
Peggy: They ________ good either. (look)
Jerry: Look at those red ones!
Peggy: They ________ good either. (look)
Emily: ________ these blue ones ________ nice? (seem)
Jerry: Let me try them on.

2. Pam: This milk ________ good. (smell)
Ed: Let me have a sip. . . . Yuck! It ________ good either. (taste)

3. Amy: Let's change the radio station. This music ________ good. (sound)
Ally: I agree. It ________ pleasant, just noisy. (seem)

4. (near the hospital cafeteria)

Mrs. Walker: Shirley, let's have lunch together today. Do you have time?
Dr. Cook: Sure, but let's go out. The cafeteria food ________ good today. (smell)
Mrs. Walker: Oh. This food ________ good either. (look)
Dr. Cook: Believe me. It ________ good. (taste)

5. Ann: Mom, how does this look? It ________ right. (feel)
Pam: Well, it ________ bad, but you want to be comfortable. (look)

6. Ed: ________ that music ________ too loud? (seem)
Ann: It ________ too loud to me. (sound)

Exercise 12 Cleaning the Refrigerator.

Use the words in parentheses to write negative questions. Fill the small blanks with short answers.

Gary, Amy, and Ally are looking in the refrigerator for something to eat.

Gary: ________ this cheese ________________ bad? (smell)

Ally: No, all blue cheese smells like that.

Gary: ________ this bread ________________ bad? (look)

Amy: Yes, it ________. It looks green. Throw it out!

Gary: ________ this melon ________________ ripe? (feel)

Ally: Yes, it ________. Let's eat it for supper.

Amy: ________ this cake ________________ old? (seem)

Gary: No, it ________. Give it to me. I'll eat it.

Amy: Here's the pie. ________ it ________________ good? (taste)

Ally: Yes, it ________. Let's have a snack. . . .

Their mother comes into the kitchen. She looks for a piece of pie. Use the positive form.

Mom: Where's the pie? There's no more pie?

Ally: You ________ hungry (seem), and you ________________ angry. (sound) Sorry, Mom. There's no more pie.

Appear is like *seem*, but it is more formal. Use *to be* or *to have* after *appear*.

Example Sentences in Context:

Jane seems tired and pale.
She appears to be sick.
She appears to have a fever.

We use *to be/to have* with *seem* too:

She seems to be sick.
She seems to have a fever.

NOTE: Do not use *to have* with adjectives.

Exercise 13 The Garcias Move In.

Use seem *or* appear *and* to be *or* to have. *Remember to use an* -s *or* -es *with subjects like* he, she, *and* it.

Gloria: This neighborhood ________________ a really nice one. (appear) The neighbors ________________ friendly. (seem)

Tony: And this house ________________ right for us. (seem) The house ________________ enough space for all of us. (seem)

Gloria: And there ________________ enough closet space. (appear)

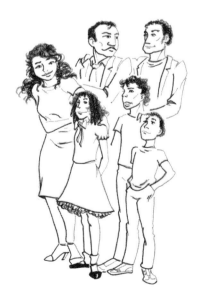

Exercise 14 What Is It?

Complete these sentences with APPEAR *or* SEEM *and* TO BE *or* TO HAVE *to complete the paragraph. Remember,* TO BE *takes adjectives, but* TO HAVE *does not.*

What is it? It ______________ an ordinary box, but it ______________ a lock on it. It ______________ very old, and it ______________ heavy. There ______________ a way to open it here. Oh, look. It ______________ an old map in the cover!

5.7 Verbs of the Senses with LIKE

Example Sentences in Context:

Ed: What's going on? It *sounds like* a party.

Pam: It *smells like* a barbecue.

Ed: There are so many cars. It *looks like* a meeting.

Pam: It *seems like* a dinner. Let's go in and find out!

All: Surprise! Happy Birthday!

Ed: Wow! This is great. I *feel like* a king, and this cake *tastes* like heaven!

Subject	Verb of Sense	LIKE	Noun
It	sounds	like	a party.
It	smells	like	a barbecue.
It	looks	like	a meeting.
It	seems	like	a dinner.
I	feel	like	a king.
This cake	tastes	like	heaven.

Exercise 15 What Does It Smell Like? Mini-Contexts.

Make sentences with the words in parentheses to answer the questions.

1. What does a baby __________ like?
   a. (smell — baby powder) ______________________
   b. (sound — a kitten) ______________________
   c. (feel — velvet) ______________________

2. What does Rosa ________ like?
   a. (look — her mother) ________________
   b. (sound — angel) ________________
   c. (smell — roses) ________________
   d. (seem — a friendly person) ________________

3. What does beef jerky ________ like?
   a. (look — leather) ________________
   b. (feel — cardboard) ________________
   c. (taste — garlic and salt) ________________

4. What does clay ________ like?
   a. (look — a stone) ________________
   b. (smells — wet earth) ________________
   c. (feel — smooth dough) ________________

5. What does a zebra ________ like?
   a. (look — a horse with stripes) ________________
   b. (sound — a monkey) ________________
   c. (feel — a donkey) ________________

6. What does charcoal ________ like?
   a. (look — coal or stones) ________________
   b. (taste — nothing at all) ________________
   c. (smell — smoke) ________________
   d. (feel — a smooth rock) ________________

7. What does cotton candy ________ like?
   a. (look — cotton) ________________
   b. (taste — pure sugar) ________________
   c. (smell — bubble gum) ________________
   d. (feel — a cloud) ________________

8. What does broccoli ________ like?
   a. (look — a little tree) ________________
   b. (taste — cabbage) ________________
   c. (smell — spinach) ________________

Exercise 16 What Does It Look Like?

Use verbs of the senses with LIKE *to answer these questions.*

Foods: What ________ like a ________?

tomato	cucumber	grapefruit	brussels sprouts
cabbage	lettuce	salad dressing	popcorn

1. What ________________ large pickle? (look)
   A ________________ does.
2. What ________________ a big yellow orange? (look)
   A ________________ does.
3. What ________________ an apple? (look)
   A ________________ does.
4. What ________________ green leaves? (taste)
   ________________ does.
5. What ________________ a heavy ball? (feel)
   A head of ________________ does.
6. What ________________ vinegar? (smell)
   ________________ does.
7. What ________________ little firecrackers in a pot? (sound)
   ________________ does.
8. What ________________ small cabbages? (seem)
   ________________ do.

Unit 6: The Simple Present Tense

WE LEARN TOGETHER.

6.1 Present Indicative *(Third Person, Singular and Plural)*

Example Sentences in Context:

Mrs. Garcia teaches the seventh grade math and science. She likes her job at Springfield Middle School. She usually goes to school at seven-thirty in the morning. She has five classes and one study hall. She sometimes stays after school. She does her lesson plans at school.

Two of Mrs. Garcia's students are Jerry Smith and Gary Walker. They have math class in the morning. They are also in Mrs. Garcia's homeroom. They ride to school on their bicycles at eight. They get there in time for the 8:15 bell.

Subject	Verb	Rest of Sentence
Mrs. Garcia	teaches	the seventh grade.
She	likes	her job.
She	goes	to school at 7:30.
She	has	five classes.
She	stays	after school.
She	does	her lesson plans.
They	have	math class.
They	ride	to school on their bikes.
They	get	there in time for the bell.

NOTE: ***He, she,* and *it* take an *-es* ending.** The spelling changes according to the first spelling of the word. (The verb doesn't change for *they*.) For most words ending in a consonant and all ending in *-e*, add only *-s*.

like → likes put → puts ride → rides kick → kicks learn → learns

For words ending in *-y* without a vowel before the *-y*, change the *-y* to *-i* and add *-es*.

fly → flies dry → dries carry → carries marry → marries

For those ending in *-y* with a vowel before the *-y*, add *-s*:

say → says play → plays stay → stays stray → strays

For all other verbs, add *-es*:

watch → watches wash → washes teach → teaches
wish → wishes kiss → kisses buzz → buzzes

Exercise 1 He Always Watches TV.

Practice writing these verbs. Change spelling if necessary.

1. He always . . .
   a. watch TV: ______________________
   b. take out the garbage: ______________________
   c. read the newspaper: ______________________
   d. go to a movie: ______________________
   e. want dinner on time: ______________________
   f. dry the dishes after supper: ______________________
   g. kiss his mom before school: ______________________
   h. kick the ball hard: ______________________

2. She usually . . .
   a. wash her hair every morning: ________________
   b. scrub the floor on Fridays: ________________
   c. cry at sad movies: ________________
   d. drive to the college: ________________
   e. bounce the ball off the wall: ________________
   f. ride her bike in the morning: ________________
   g. play golf on Saturdays: ________________
3. They never . . .
   a. make mistakes: ________________
   b. cut class: ________________
   c. fight on the playground: ________________
   d. fix anything: ________________

Exercise 2 The Garcia Family.

Complete these sentences. Maybe the verb will change, but the verb may not change.

The Garcia family ________ (live) in Springfield. They ________ (live) in a house on Fourth Avenue. Their house ________ (be) in the same neighborhood as the Smiths', the Clarks', and the Walkers'.

Dr. Garcia ________ (be) a dentist. He ________ (drive) to his office near the mall. He ________ (see) patients five days a week. He ________ (work) Mondays, Tuesdays, Thursdays, Fridays, and Saturdays. He ________ (take) Wednesdays off.

Mrs. Garcia ________ (teach) math and science at the middle school. Dr. and Mrs. Garcia ________ (have) four children. John ________ (go) to Taylor College. He ________ (study) science. He ________ (want) to be a dentist like his father. Andy ________ (attend) Springfield High School. Andy ________ (swim) on the high school swim team. Rosa ________ (be) in the sixth grade. She ________ (like) music a lot. Tommy ________ (go) to Springfield Elementary School. He ________ (play) soccer on Saturdays. They are a busy family.

Exercise 3 Dr. Garcia.

Complete the sentences. Use the verbs in parentheses.

Dr. Garcia ________ (have) an office on Maple Street. He ________ (stand) on his feet all day long. He ________ (check) people's teeth, ________ (clean) teeth, and ________ (fix) teeth. People ________ (like) Dr. Garcia. He is a kind and gentle person.

6.2 The Simple Present Tense *(First and Second Person, Singular and Plural)*

Example Sentences in Context:

John is talking with Ann Clark, outside the new Garcia house.

John: Hi, Ann.

Ann: Welcome to the neighborhood, John. This is a nice place to live. Are you going to Taylor College this fall?

John: Yes, I'm taking chemistry, German, humanities, and calculus. How about you?

Ann: I'm in Dr. Hunter's Math 101 class, and I'm also taking English composition, geology, and history.

John: That sounds like a full schedule. How do you get to school?

Ann: Three of us drive to school together. Do you want to join our carpool?

John: Yes, I do. Carpooling sounds good to me. When do you leave?

Ann: We leave at 7:30 for first hour classes, and we come home at 4:00. I study in the library between classes. I don't have classes after 1:00.

Subject	Verb	Rest of Sentence
That	sounds	like a full schedule.
Three of us	drive	to school together.
I	do.	
I	don't have	classes after 1:00.
Carpooling	sounds	good to me.
We	leave	at 7:30.
We	come	home at 4:00.
I	study	in the library between classes.
(Do) you	want	to join our carpool?
(How do) you	get	to school?

Exercise 4 At Dr. Garcia's Office.

Fill in the blanks with the simple present tense form of the verb in parentheses.

George Smith ________ (have) a dental checkup today, so he ________ (go) to see Dr. Tony Garcia. He ________ (arrive) at Dr. Garcia's office at 12:55. He ________ (see) the dentist at 1:00.

The receptionist ________ (ask) him to fill out an insurance form. Then she ________ (take) him to an examination room. She ________ (put) a bib on him, and then she ________ (arrange) the dental instruments on a tray for the dentist. The receptionist and Mr. Smith ________ (talk) about the weather and the Taylor College football team. Then Dr. Garcia ________ (come) in. The receptionist ________ (leave), and the exam ________ (begin).

Dr. Garcia: Well, George, let's have a look!

Mr. Smith: ________ you ________ (see) anything?

Dr. Garcia: Well, I ________n't ________ (see) any cavities.

Mr. Smith: That's good. I always ________ (brush) my teeth, and I ________ (use) dental floss every day.

Dr. Garcia: Good, good. Your teeth ________ (look) clean, but let's take some x-rays.

Exercise 5 Saturday Morning at the Garcia's.

Fill in the blanks with the simple present tense form of the verb in parentheses. Remember: use the present tense form for habits and schedules.

It's Saturday morning at the Garcia's house. Everyone ________ (clean); everyone ________ (help). Rosa ________ (wash) the laundry in the washing machine. She ________ (dry) it in the clothes dryer. Then she ________ (fold) the clothes and ________ (put) all of the clothes away.

Tommy ________ (vacuum) all the rugs and ________ (take) out the trash. He ________ (dust) the furniture, and once a month he ________ (polish) it too.

Andy ________ (sweep) the kitchen floor, ________ (scrub) it with soap and water, and then he ________ (wax) the floor.

John ________ (mow) the lawn, ________ (rake) up the leaves and dry grass, and ________ (put) them in large plastic bags. He also ________ (water) the lawn and ________ (clean) the flower beds.

Mrs. Garcia ________ (clean) the kitchen. She ________ (wipe) out the refrigerator and ________ (wipe) off the stove. She ________ (write) out a grocery list. She also ________ (iron) Dr. Garcia's white shirts.

In the afternoon, Dr. Garcia ________ (come) home from his office. He ________ (wash) the car and then ________ (wax) it. He also ________ (check) the oil in the motor. He ________ (look) at the battery to be sure of the water level. He also ________ (test) the air pressure in the tires.

They ________ (finish) the work at about 3:00. Then they all ________ (go) out.

Exercise 6 Lots to Do. Mini-Contexts.

Fill in the blanks with the simple present tense form of the verb in parentheses.

1. Carpooling ________ (be) an American custom. Several people ________ (travel) to work or to school together in one car. They ________ (save) money. They ________ (ride) together. Each person ________ (pay) part of the gasoline bill.

2. Ann: ________ n't you ________ (have) an eight o'clock class?
   John: Yes, I ________.
   Ann: Why ________ n't you ________ (come) to my house just before 7:30 tomorrow?
   John: OK! See you then.

3. Andy: Rosa, you ________ n't ________ (have) much to do. ________ n't you ________ (want) to help your brother?
   Rosa: No, I ________ n't. You ________ n't ________ (have) much to do. And I ________! There are six loads of laundry to fold.

4. Jerry: ________ you ________ (have) your math homework?
   Gary: It ________ (be) here in my backpack. ________ you ________ (need) some help with it?
   Jerry: I sure ________. ________ you ________ (understand) it?
   Gary: Yes, I ________. My dad always ________ (help) me with math. Let me help you.

Exercise 7 Amy and Allison.

Practice with first and second person.

Amy: What time ________ we ________ (play) tennis on Saturday?

Allison: Eleven o'clock. I think.

Amy: We ________ (start) on Court A.

Allison: ________ we ________ (have) a ride, or ________ we ________ (ride) our bicycles?

Amy: Let's ask Mom. Maybe she ________ (have) time to take us.

6.3 Present Time in Questions with Question Words

Example Sentences in Context:

Where does the parade go?	It starts at the mall, goes down Grand Street to 6th Avenue, then down Main Street to the park.
When does it start?	At nine-thirty.
How often does Springfield have a parade?	Once a year on the Fourth of July.
What time does the parade end?	About eleven o'clock.
Who leads the parade?	The mayor does, in a big white car with an open top.
What is the Fourth of July parade?	It's a birthday party for the country.
What does the mayor do?	He waves his hat and smiles. After the parade, he gives a speech at the park.

Summary

Question Word	Helping Word	Subject	Verb	Rest of Sentence
Where	does	the parade	go?	
When	does	it	start?	
How often	does	Springfield	have	a parade?
What time	does	the parade	end?	
What	does	the mayor	do?	

NOTE: *Who* and *What* sometimes take the place of the subject.

Subject (Question Word)	Verb	Rest of Sentence
Who	leads	the parade?
What	is	a Fourth of July parade?

Exercise 8 Who Is That? Mini-Contexts.

These are some of the people of Springfield. They all have important jobs. Finish the questions and answers with the verbs in parentheses.

1. Bob: That is Ann Clark, a college student.

Dan: What ________ she ________ (study)?

Bob: She ________ (study) math.**

Dan: Where ________ she ________ work?

Bob: She ________ (work) at the Taylor College cafeteria.

Dan: How often ________ she ________ (work) there?

Bob: Two or three days a week.

** Use the BE + Verb + -ing to mean "Math is her major."

2. Bob: That is George Smith.

Dan: What ________ he ________ (do)?

Bob: He ________ (run) the Maple Leaf Supermarkets in Springfield.

Dan: How many stores ________ he ________ (manage)?

Bob: Three.

3. Bob: That is Jerry Smith. He ________ (enjoy) baseball.
   Dan: How often ________ he ________ (play)?
   Bob: Three or four times a week in the summertime.
   Dan: When ________ (be) their games?
   Bob: Usually late in the afternoon.

4. Bob: That is Pamela Clark.
   Dan: What ________ (be) her job?
   Bob: She ________ (be) a lawyer.
   Dan: Where ________ she ________ (work)?
   Bob: She ________ (have) an office downtown, near city hall.
   Dan: How often ________ she ________ (go) to court?
   Bob: Several times a week.

5. Bob: That is Fred Hanson of the Hanson Brothers Moving Company. He and his brother Frank ________ (own) a big truck.
   Dan: What ________ they ________ (use) the truck for?
   Bob: They ________ (help) people to move. They ________ (move) a houseful of furniture to a new house.
   Dan: How often ________ they ________ (rent) out their truck?
   Bob: Sometimes every day.

6. Bob: Buck Nelson is a mechanic.
   Dan: What ________ a mechanic ________ (do)?
   Bob: He ________ (fix) cars at a garage.
   Dan: Where ________ Buck ________ (work)?
   Bob: At Buck's Car Repair.
   Dan: Where ________ (be) it?
   Bob: At the corner of Prospect and College Streets.
   Dan: Who ________ (own) it?
   Bob: Buck, of course.

7. Ed: Where ________ you ________ (work) today?

Pam: At court.

Ed: When ________ the trial ________ (start)?

Pam: About nine o'clock.

Ed: How ________ you ________ (feel) about the case?

Pam: I ________ (feel) OK. I'm not sure about my client.

Ed: Who ________ (be) your client?

Pam: Joan Larson.

Ed: ________ she ________ (run) Triangle Realty?

Pam: That's the one.

6.4 Simple Present Tense with Negatives *(Statements and Questions)*

Jason travels to New York for TTT Electronics. He always goes first class. He does company work on the airplane, so he needs the extra space.

Jason is checking in at the airline ticket counter. He is talking with Pete Robinson, the airline representative.

Pete: Yes, sir?

Jason: I need information about a flight to New York. When does the next flight leave?

Pete: In about 50 minutes. Do you have a ticket?

Jason: No, and I need a round-trip ticket. I want to return on Friday.

Pete: Do you want first class or coach?

Jason: First class, please. I don't want to be crowded.

Pete: Do you want a window seat?

Jason: No, I don't. I prefer an aisle seat.

Pete: Where do you want to sit, smoking or non-smoking?

Jason: I don't smoke, so let me sit in the first row.

Pete: I'm sorry. We don't have an empty aisle seat in Row 1.

Jason: Don't you have an empty aisle seat in first class?

Pete: Just a moment. . . . Yes, we do. Is an aisle seat in Row 3 OK?

Jason: Yes, it is. That's fine.

Pete: How do you want to pay for your ticket?

Jason: Here's my credit card.

Pete: Thank you.

Jason: What gate do I go to please? And what is the flight number?

Pete: It's Flight number 262. It departs from Gate 3 at 2:45. Do you have any baggage to check?

Jason: No, I don't. Just this carry-on bag.

Pete: Here's your ticket. Have a nice trip.

Jason: Thanks!

Statements

Subject	Do + Not	Verb	Rest of Sentence
I	don't	want	to be crowded.
We	don't	have	an empty aisle seat.
Yes, I		do.	
Yes, we		do.	
No, I	don't.		
No, we	don't.		

Questions

Do + Not	Subject	Verb	Rest of Sentence
Don't	you	have	an empty aisle seat?

More Example Sentences in Context:

Jason calls his wife from the airport.

Jason: (on the phone) Sara, I *don't* have much time. The flight leaves in half an hour.
Sara: Does it go direct to New York?
Jason: No, it *doesn't.* They don't have any direct flights in the afternoon.
Sara: Do you have time to get something to eat?
Jason: *Don't* they serve dinner on the plane?
Sara: I *don't* think so.

Subject	Do + Not	Verb	Rest of Sentence
It	doesn't.		
They	don't	have	any direct flights.

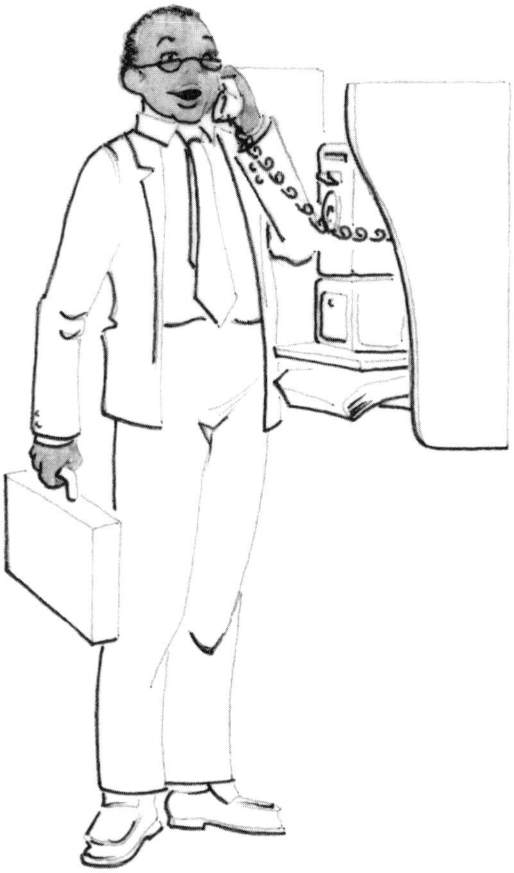

Exercise 9
On the Plane. Mini-Contexts.

Use the verb in the parentheses in a positive (+) or negative (—) sense to complete these sentences or questions. Remember to use do *in questions.*

1. On the plane, the flight attendant asks Jason a question:

   Flight Attendant: ________ something to drink, sir? (want +)

   Jason: Yes, some grapefruit juice, please.

   Flight Attendant: Oh, I'm sorry. We ________ any grapefruit juice. (have —) We have apple, orange, and tomato juice.

   Jason: I ________ any of those. (like —) ________ (have +) a Coke?

   Flight Attendant: Yes.

2. Flight Attendant: We have some choices for dinner: baked chicken, steak, or spaghetti.

   Jason: Oh, I'm not very hungry. ________ something light? (have +)

   Flight Attendant: Let me check. . . . We have a vegetarian plate.

3. Student: Dr. Clark? I'm a new student in your class.

   Dr. Clark: Why ________ a seat now? (take —) And come to my office after class. . . .

   Student: I have a class right after yours, so I ________ time until three o'clock. (have —)

   Dr. Clark: Why ________ come to my office then? (come —)

4. Mrs. Smith is talking to her family at the dinner table.

   Emily: George, ________ some carrots? (want —)

   George: I ate some, dear. I ________ any more. (want —)

   Emily: Jerry, ________ the potatoes? (like —)

   Jerry: No, I'm full. I ________ any more. (want —)

   Emily: Ricky, ________ to eat your peas? (want —)

   Peggy: No, Mom. He ________. (do —) He isn't eating the peas on his plate.

NOTE: In English, we sometimes use the negative question form *(Why don't you . . . ?)* for a suggestion.

It's raining, and it's cold.
Put on your coat.: Why don't you put on your coat?
Take some gloves.: Why don't you take some gloves?
Wear your hat.: Why don't you wear your hat?

Exercise 10 It's Hot!

Change the commands to polite requests.

1. Get a hat. ______________________________
2. Put on your shoes. ______________________________
3. Get your bathing suit. ______________________________
4. Have a cold drink. ______________________________
5. Take off your sweater. ______________________________
6. Open the window. ______________________________
7. Turn on the fan. ______________________________
8. Go for a swim. ______________________________

6.5 Adverbs of Frequency with Verbs in Simple Present Time *(See Unit 4.3)*

Example Sentences in Context:

Sara Walker always gets up early.
She frequently jogs before breakfast.
She usually fixes breakfast for the family.
She often has time to talk with her husband before breakfast.
She sometimes makes pancakes.
She seldom leaves before eight o'clock.
She rarely has a meeting before nine.
She never gets to work late.

NOTE: The adverbs of frequency come before the verb (but often after a *be* verb). With a negative, the adverb of frequency follows *don't* or *doesn't.*

I don't always get up early.
I don't often jog in the morning.
Jason doesn't usually drink coffee.
They don't ever sleep late.

Exercise 11 Emily Goes Shopping.

Write these sentences again. Use the adverb in parentheses.

1. Emily goes shopping on Wednesdays. (always)

   ____

2. She takes Peggy with her. (usually)

   ____

3. They take Ricky with them. (never)

   ____

4. They go to the market on Oak Street (sometimes), but they go to the market on Hospital Parkway. (rarely)

   ____

   ____

5. Emily and Peggy leave home for the store at three o'clock. (often)

   ____

6. Peggy arrives home from school just before three. (usually)

   ____

7. On the way home, they pick up Jerry at the ball park. (frequently)

   ____

8. They get home before five o'clock. (seldom)

____

9. They buy groceries for a week. (usually)

____

10. George puts the groceries away. (sometimes)

____

Exercise 12 Frequently Asked Questions About Me.

Answer these questions about yourself. Use adverbs of frequency.

1. *Q:* How often do you go to the movies?
   A: I go ____________. ____________ times a ____________. (week, month)

2. *Q:* How frequently do you get a haircut?
   A: ____________, about ____________

3. *Q:* Do you ever eat lobster?
   A: ____________

4. *Q:* How often do you visit your dentist for a check-up?
   A: ____________

5. *Q:* How often do you go out to eat?
   A: ____________

6. *Q:* How frequently do you swim?
   A: ____________

7. *Q:* How often do you exercise?
   A: ____________

8. *Q:* How frequently do you visit your family?
   A: ____________

9. *Q:* How often do you cook for ten or more people?
   A: ____________

10. *Q:* Do you ever sing?
    A: ____________

Exercise 13 The Tennis Schedule.

How often do these people play? Rewrite the sentences.

1. The Clarks play tennis every day at 5 o'clock. They play tennis at 5 o'clock. (always)

   ____

2. The O'Neills play three times a week. They play early in the morning. (usually)

   ____

3. The Springers don't have much time for tennis. They play early in the morning. (usually)

   ____

4. The Clarks play tennis nearly every day. They play tennis. (frequently)

   ____

5. Dr. Cook has Wednesdays and Saturday afternoons off. She plays tennis then. (often)

   ____

6. Dan Billings works out of town most of the time. He plays tennis. (rarely)

   ____

7. All lessons are in the schedule for eleven and one o'clock. (always)

   ____

8. There are only lessons in the late morning and early afternoon. There are lessons at night. (never)

   ____

9. The tennis teacher usually uses Court B for lessons. She uses Court A. (seldom)

   ____

10. Jim Charles plays once a week at most. He plays tennis. (seldom)

    ____

Now make your own choices. Rewrite the first sentence with an adverb of frequency. Which adverb fits best?

11. The Newcombs play tennis.They play on Mondays, Tuesdays, and Saturdays.

    ____

12. Pat Flanagan plays tennis. He only plays on Saturdays.

    ____

13. Dr. Fronski plays on his days off, Wednesdays and Saturdays.

    ____

14. The Andersons play on Court A on weekdays.

____

15. The Springers play on the same court two days in a row.

____

16. Dr. Fronski and Dr. Cook play tennis on Fridays. (They work at the hospital on Fridays.)

____

17. The Chens play at one o'clock and three o'clock. (They play at different times.)

____

18. There are some free times on both courts on Thursday afternoons.

____

19. The Hanson brothers play tennis in the late afternoon.

____

20. Tom Turner doesn't have classes on Wednesday and Thursday afternoons, so he plays tennis then.

____

Unit 7: Past Time

WE ENJOYED THE MOVIE LAST NIGHT.

7.1 Simple Past Time

Example Sentences in Context:

What kind of child was I?
I liked movies then, and I still like them now.
I enjoyed games then, and I still enjoy them.
I watched TV a lot then, and I still do now.
I didn't listen to other people very well then, and I still don't.
My mother pointed out all my faults then, and she still does.
I was a difficult person then, and I still am.

Grammar Note: There are three ways to pronounce the *-ed*, but only one way to spell it.

liked /laykt/ has a final *t* sound.
enjoyed /ənjoyd/ has a final *d*, sound.
pointed /poyntəd/ has an *-ed* sound at the end.

The spelling of *-ed* always looks the same. Sometimes the spelling of the whole verb changes.

1. **Add *-ed*:**

Some verbs end in two vowels and one consonant: **wait** **need** **rain**
Or two consonants: **count** **point** **list**
Or a vowel and a ***y***: **enjoy** **play** **stay**

To verbs like these, add *-ed*.

Examples:

It *rained.* I *waited.* I *needed* an umbrella.

The children *listed* the books. They *counted* the mysteries. They *pointed* out the best ones.

They *stayed* at the party. The children *played* games. Their parents *enjoyed* it too.

2. **Change the *-y* to *-i*. Then add *-ed:***

Some verbs end in a consonant or two and a ***-y***: **try** **study** **worry**

Change the verb like these examples:

Last night I *worried* about my math test. I *tried* to study for several hours. I *studied* some more today.

3. **Add *-d***

Some verbs end in ***-e***: **shave** **smile** **like**

Add just a *-d* to these verbs. (The *-e* is there already.)

Examples:

The man *shaved* off his beard. Then he *smiled.* He *liked* it.

NOTE: This final *e* is called a "silent *e*." It makes a vowel "long." A long vowel in English says its own name.

4. **Double the consonant and add *-ed:***

Some verbs have one vowel and one consonant at the end: **jog** **stop** **nap**
We can't add just *-ed*. (The vowel must be short, not long. The *-e* of the *-d* cannot look like a "silent *e*.")

So we double the consonant.

Examples:

Joe *jogged* with Tom. They *stopped* after an hour. Tom *jogged* home, but Joe walked home slowly. Then he *napped* for an hour and was late for school.

Exercise 1 They Listened to the Radio. Mini-Contexts.

Fill the blanks with the correct spelling of the past tense verb.

1. The movie (start) ________________ at seven o'clock. It (finish) ________________ at nine. We (watch) ________________ the whole thing and (enjoy) ________________ it a lot. We all (laugh) ________ at the funny parts. Everyone (cry) ________ at the end. Then we (turn) ________ the TV set off. We (talk) ________ about the movie later, and we (decide) ________________ to go for a walk.
2. This morning it ________________ (rain). I ________________ (want) to play tennis at the Country Club, but it was too wet. I ________________ (stay) in bed until eleven o'clock. Then I ________________ (fix) myself some breakfast, and I ________________ (enjoy) some peace and quiet at home.
3. Amy and Allison ________________ (listen) carefully to the weather report. They (wait) for the sports news too. They ________________ (want) the results of the high school football games.

> *NOTE:* The question form and negatives follow the usual rules: See 7.3. There are no changes for *we, you, they, he, she,* or *it*:
>
> You liked to get to school early.
> We walked to school together.
> Tommy tagged along with us, and he tried to keep up.
> Our friend waited for us near the park.

Exercise 2 Joe Anderson.

Change the verb in the first part of the sentence to make a past tense sentence.

1. I pull myself out of bed at seven o'clock every morning, and I ________________ myself out of bed at seven yesterday.
2. I jog for half an hour every morning, and yesterday I ________________ too.
3. I shower every day, and I ________________ yesterday too.
4. I wash my hair every morning, and I ________ my hair yesterday.

5. I shave every morning, and I ________________ yesterday.*
6. I cook breakfast every day, and I ________________ breakfast yesterday.
7. I fix orange juice every day, and I ________________ orange juice yesterday.
8. I brush my teeth every morning, and I ________________ my teeth yesterday.
9. I stop to plan a schedule every day, and I ________________ to plan my schedule yesterday.
10. I usually do all these things, but today I ________________n't. I stayed in bed until noon.

* He shaves and trims his beard.

What did Joe Anderson do yesterday?

Yesterday Joe ____

____

____

____

What does Joe Anderson usually do?

____

____

____

What didn't Joe do this morning?

____

____

____

____

Ask one of your classmates: What did you do this morning?

This morning my classmate . . .

____

____

____

____

____

____

____

____

____

7.2 Past Time Expressions

Simple past time words: *then, yesterday*

Past time expressions with *yesterday*:

yesterday morning

yesterday afternoon

yesterday evening

Expressions with *last*:

last evening
last night
last week
last month
last year
last Tuesday
last January
last spring, summer, fall, winter
last semester
last term

Expressions with *ago*:

an hour ago
a day ago
a month ago
a week ago
two months ago
a year ago
ten years ago

Exercise 3 Where Were You a Minute Ago?

Write out full answers. Use the BE *verb.*

Where were you ____________________?

1. *I was in the classroom* a minute ago.
2. ________________________ an hour ago.
3. ________________________ last summer.
4. ________________________ last December.
5. ________________________ yesterday morning.

What did you do ______________?

6. ______________ (laugh at a silly joke, a minute ago)
7. ______________ (cook lunch, an hour ago)
8. ______________ (enjoy a movie on TV, last night)
9. ______________ (watch a baseball game, yesterday evening)
10. ______________ (hunt for a lost notebook, yesterday afternoon)
11. ______________ (work for my dad, last summer)
12. ______________ (want to earn some money, last semester); so

    ______________ (sign up for a job.)

Exercise 4
"Love of Reading Week."

Use the verbs in parentheses to complete the sentences.

Tommy is in Mrs. Watson's class. Last week was "Love of Reading Week."

1. Last Monday, they ________ a chart to list all their books. (design)
2. The children ________ all of their mystery books last Monday. (count)
3. They ________ all of their books a week ago. (list)
4. Last Tuesday they ________ the story of George Washington. (finish) They ________ about a lot of famous people. (study)
5. They ________ to make a list of biographies last week. (start)
6. A week ago, Mrs. Watson ________ the children how to play an old American party-game. (show)
7. She ________ Tommy with a handkerchief. (blindfold)
8. Then she ________ him around and around. (turn)
9. He ________ to pin a paper tail on a picture of a donkey. (try)
10. The children ________ a lot about American culture last week. (learn)
11. They ________ a lot of games and ________ to many folk stories. (play, listen)
12. Then last Friday Mrs. Watson ________ them make a big poster. (help)

Exercise 5 The Hike.

Write the sentences in order. Use the clue words. Don't forget to change the verb if necessary.

1. Last summer / hike / I / in the mountains

   ____

2. My brother and I / climb / to 10,000 feet

   ____

3. camp / We / in the woods

   ____

4. It / one night / rain

   ____

5. cook / our dinner / We / that night / in a cave

   ____

6. stay / too / in the cave / We / all night

   ____

7. We / alone / were not

   ____

8. share the cave / four raccoons / We / two rabbits / and lots of mosquitoes

   ____

Example Sentences in Context:

On an airplane.

A: Did you enjoy the movie?

B: What movie?

A: Didn't you watch the movie?

B: No, I didn't watch the movie.

A: Did you take a nap?

B: Perhaps I did.

A: Yes, you did, and you did something else!

B: What did I do?

A: You missed a great movie.

(Question Word Order)	Subject	Verb	Rest of Sentence
Did	you	enjoy	the movie?
Didn't	you	watch	the movie?
	No, I	didn't watch	a movie.
What did	I	do?	
(Short)	Perhaps I	did.	
(Answers)	You	did.	

Grammar Note: There are no changes for *I, we, you, they, he, she, it.* The full form is *did not.* Use *did not* for a strong negative answer:

A: You did it!

B: No, I did *not*!

Exercise 6 Where Is Your Homework?

Use the clue words in parentheses to complete the sentences. All verbs should be in past time. To give a strong negative answer, use did not.

Part A

Mrs. Watson: Tommy, where is your homework?

Tommy: Our dog ________________ it into a hundred pieces. (rip)

Mrs. Watson: He ________________ ________________! Where is it?

Tommy: My dad ________________ it up with his papers. (pick) It's at his office.

Mrs. Watson: He ________________ ________________! Where is it?

Tommy: My mom ________________ her coffee on it. (spill)

Mrs. Watson: She ________________ ________________! Where is it?

Tommy: My sister Rosa ________________ up all the paper and pencils in the house. (use)

Mrs. Watson: She ________________ ________________! Tommy, you ________________ do it, ________________ you?

Tommy: No, I ________________.

Part B

Mrs. Watson: Tommy's dog ________________ ________________ his homework. (eat) His dad ________________ ________________ it up with his papers. (pick) His mother ________________ ________________ her coffee on it. (spill) His sister ________________ ________________ up all the paper and pencils in the house. (use) Tommy ________________ ________________ his homework. (do)

Exercise 7 Bill Henderson's Summer.

Write out the rest of the sentence. Follow the example.

Part A

1. Last summer Bill wanted to play a lot of sports. Bill says:

   a. I wanted to play golf, but I ___didn't___ ___play___ much at all.

   b. I wanted to play tennis, but I ________ ________ much at all. I ________ ________ a partner.

   c. I wanted to ride a horse, but I ________ ________ any horses at all. It was too expensive.

   d. I wanted to play basketball, but it was too hot. So I ________ ________ basketball at all.

   e. I wanted to go surfing on the ocean, but we stayed home. I ________ ________ surfing at all.

   f. I wanted to jog, but my knees hurt too much. I ________ ________ at all.

   g. I ________ want to ride my bicycle. I use my bicycle to go to school, but I ________! (like to)

Part B

Write a paragraph. Tell what Bill didn't do.

Bill: ____

____

____

____

____

____

____

____

____

____

____

____

____

____

____

Exercise 8 Did You, or Didn't You?

Use short answers: Yes, I did./No, I didn't.

1. Sara Did you go to the telephone company?
Jason: Yes, ________.
Sara: Did you do the shopping?
Jason: No, I ________.
Sara: Didn't you get anything for supper?
Jason: No, ________. Let's go out to eat.

2. Ed: Did you go the the paint store today?
Pam: Yes, ________.
Ed: Did you remember to buy new brushes?
Pam: Yes, ________. And did you buy some plastic to cover the furniture?
Ed: Oops! No, ________.

3. Tony: Tomorrow is my mother's birthday. Did you send her a card?
Gloria: No, ________. Did you?
Tony: No, ________. Let's send her some flowers.

4. Tommy: Where is my new notebook, Mom? Did you get me one?
Mother: Oh, Tommy, no, I ________. I didn't remember at all.
Tommy: I need it to do my homework for tomorrow for science.
Mother: Let me go to the store now to get it. Why don't you start your science now?
Tommy: OK. . . . Oh. Where is my science book?
Mother: Didn't you bring it home?
Tommy: No, I ________.

5. Emily: Ricky, let's go to the park.
Ricky: No.
Emily: Didn't you like the park last week?
Ricky: No, I ________.

6. Ann: Did you sign up for math for next semester?
Bill: No, I ________. Didn't you decide not to take math?
Ann: Yes, I ________, but I changed my mind.
Bill: Well, I ________.
Ann: That's too bad. Why don't you sign up now?
Bill: OK.

Example Sentences in Context:

Tony Garcia was in the Public Health Service for three years. He was a young dentist there, and he traveled a lot. He always worked with poor people. He usually stayed a week in each place. He frequently pulled teeth one week and fitted false teeth a month later. He often worked six days a week. He sometimes worked for ten or twelve hours a day. He seldom had a day off. He rarely watched television in those days, and he never wasted time. He gained a lot of experience in those three years.

Subject	Adverb of Frequency	Verb	Rest of Sentence
He	always	worked	with poor people.
He	usually	stayed	a week in each place.
He	frequently	pulled	teeth.
He	often	worked	six days a week.
He	sometimes	worked	ten hours a day.
He	seldom	had	a day off.
He	rarely	watched	television.
(The following sentences mean the same thing.)			
He	never	wasted	time.
He	didn't ever	waste	time.

Grammar Note: The adverb of frequency with past time is like the adverb of frequency with present time. Short answers to questions with these adverbs follow this pattern:

Amy: Did he (usually) go?
Ally: Yes, he usually did.

Exercise 9 Questions About Tony Garcia.

Answer these questions about Tony's years in the Public Health Service. Give short answers. Use the adverb of frequency in your answer.

1. *Q:* Did Tony work with poor people?
   A: Yes, ______________________.
2. *Q:* Did Tony pull teeth?
   A: Yes, ______________________.
3. *Q:* Did Tony stay a few days in each place?
   A: Yes, ______________________.
4. *Q:* Did Tony have days off?
   A: ______________________
5. *Q:* Did he work on Saturdays?
   A: ______________________
6. *Q:* Did Tony watch television?
   A: ______________________
7. *Q:* Did Tony ever waste time?
   A: ______________________
8. *Q:* Did Tony work more than six hours a day?
   A: ______________________
9. *Q:* Did Tony sometimes fit people with false teeth?
   A: ______________________

Exercise 10 What Did You Do in the City?

Pretend you lived in a big city like New York, Toronto, or Paris. You did many exciting things: visiting museums, enjoying meals in fancy restaurants, seeing shows. Now answer these questions. What did you do frequently, always, sometimes, . . . ?

1. *Q:* Did you eat in restaurants?
   A: ____________________

2. *Q:* Which restaurant did you usually go to?
   A: ____________________

3. *Q:* Did you go to any shows?
   A: ____________________

4. *Q:* Did you visit the zoo?
   A: ____________________

5. *Q:* Did you go to museums?
   A: ____________________

6. *Q:* Did you go swimming?
   A: ____________________

7. *Q:* Did you take a college course?
   A: ____________________

8. *Q:* Did you go for long walks?
   A: ____________________

9. *Q:* Did you ride horses?
   A: ____________________

10. *Q:* Did you go shopping?
    A: ____________________

11. *Q:* Did you use the public library?
    A: ____________________

12. *Q:* Did you go the ball games?
    A: ____________________

Exercise 11 Mrs. Watson's Third Grade Class.

Use expressions like these in the list to make your own paragraph. Change the verbs to past tense.

listen to stories	talk during class	raise hands to answer questions
erase the board	play games with them	leave early
stay after school	rip their books	do their homework
walk around the classroom		

Last year Mrs. Watson's third grade classroom was a busy place. The students frequently ________________. They rarely ________________. Mrs. Watson sometimes ________________. The children always ________________. They often ________________. The students never ________________. They usually ________________. And they seldom ________________.

7.5 Past Continuous Time

Example Sentences in Context:

Ann: Mom, Dad just called. He needs a ride home. His car stopped on Campbell Avenue.

Pam: What happened? Did he say?

Ann: He *was driving* home, and the motor just stopped.

Pam: *Was* the motor *making* funny noises?

Ann: Mom, you know his car. The motor always makes funny noises.

Pam: OK. Let me finish this.

Ann: Mom, let's go now. Dad *wasn't sounding* very happy.

Question Word Order

Question Word	Subject	Was/Where Verb + *-ing*		Rest of Sentence
	He	was	driving	home.
Was	the motor	—	making	funny noises?
	Dad	wasn't	sounding	very happy.

Exercise 12 Tell Me All About It. Mini-Contexts.

Use the verb in parentheses to complete the sentences.

1. Rosa Mama — a — a!

Mother: What's wrong, Rosa? Why are you crying?

Rosa: I ________________ (walk) home, and Lucy called to me. I ________________n't ________________ (look) at the sidewalk and . . .

Mother: Yes, Rosa, what happened?

Rosa: I________________n't________________(pay attention) and there was a big crack in the cement. I tripped and skinned my knee. I ________________ (bleed) all the way home!

2. Jason: How was your game today, son?

Gary: It was bad. We ________________ (win) in the eighth inning. We had three runs. We ________________ (hit) every ball. We ________________ (catch) every one of theirs. We ________________ (run) really fast. Our pitcher ________________ (throw) his best game ever.

Jason: Yes, then what happened?

Gary: Three of their men were on base, and they ________________ (wait), then I did it.

Jason: What?

Gary: I ________________ (run) after a ball, and I fell. They all scored, and we lost the game.

3. Tommy: Dad! Come quick! There's a fire on Main Street. I ________________ (ride) my bike, and I heard the fire engines. I went over to Main Street. Smoke ________________ (come) from the roof of the newspaper office. The flames ________________ (go) high in the air. People ________________ (run) out of the office. One man ________________ (try) to move his car!

Tony: ________________ the firemen ________________ (do) anything?

Tommy: They ________________ (drive) to the building on the truck. They ________________ (come) to fight the fire. I wanted to tell you. So let's go, Dad!

4. Gloria: Where were you?

Tony: We ________________ (watch) the firefighters downtown. The newspaper office ________________ (burn).

Tommy: What a fire! The firefighters ________________ (set up) ladders. Some others ________________ (hook up) the hoses. One woman ________________ (climb) down the fire escape. And then, they started spraying the building. Then it ________________ (smoke) all over the place.

Tony: And we ________________ (cough), so we decided to come home.

Exercise 13 At the Customs Office.

Fill in the blanks with past tense forms.

Customs Officer: ________ you ________ (buy) anything to bring home?

Tourist: Yes, ________.

Customs Officer: ________ you ________ (buy) any meat products?

Tourist: No, ________.

Customs Officer: How much ________ you ________ (spend) on your trip?

Tourist: I don't know.

Customs Officer: How much ________ you ________ (take) with you?

Tourist: About $300.

Customs Officer: ________ you ________ (use) it all?

Tourist: No, I still have a hundred.

Exercise 14 Pam Tells Ed About Her Day in Court.

Pam: Boy, am I tired!

Ed: What happened? Was it a bad day?

Pam: You said it! Things ________________ (go) along just fine, but then I went to court.

Ed: Yes? What happened?

Pam: The judge ________________ (complain) about his case load. He ________________ (try) to get order in the courtroom. My client ________________ (worry) about some silly details. And I got a phone call. It was from my sister.

Ed: What did she want?

Pam: She ________________ (drive) home from work, and someone hit her car.

Ed: What? Is she OK?

Pam: Well, she ________________ (cry) on the telephone, but she's OK now and she needs a lawyer.

Ed: Why?

Pam: The other driver has no insurance. So, my sister ________________ (worry) about her car.

Ed: Is there a way to help her?

Pam: I'm sure.

Ed: I'm glad that she's all right. . . . But now what happened in court?

Pam: Well, I ________________ (say) . . . the judge ________________n't ________________ (feel) well. So he called it off for today. And I ________________ (count on) finishing today. Oh, well!

Exercise 15 Jimmy Brown's Life.

Look at the chart below and complete the sentences. Use past time and ago. (see 7.2)

1965	1975	1983	1987	1990	Last week	Now
Born in Ohio	Moved to Springfield	Graduated from High School	Graduated from Taylor College	Got married	Daughter was Born	

1. Jimmy Brown was born ________________ years ________________.
2. His family moved to Springfield ________________ years ________________.
3. ________________ years ________________ from high school.

4. ________________ years ________________ from Taylor College.

5. He ________________ in 1990. That was ________________ years ________________.

6. His daughter ________________ week ________________.

Exercise 16 Dan Finds a New Job.

Fill in the blanks with verbs and past time expressions.

January

1	2	3	4	5	6	7
8	9	10	11	12	13	14
15	16	17	18	19	20	21
22	23	24	25	26	27	28
29	30	31				

February

			1	2	3	4
5	6	7	8	9	10	11
12	13	14	15	16	17	18
19	20	21	22	23	24	25
26	27	28				

Jan. 2 —lost job
Jan. 5 —told parents
Jan. 7 —moved to parents' house
Jan. 24—found a new job
Jan. 26—moved back to Springfield
Feb. 2 —started new job
Feb. 3 —wrote to his parents

Today is February 5th. Dan lost his job ________________. He ________________ his parents ________________. He ________________ ________________ their house ________________. Dan ________________ back to Springfield ________________. ________________ he ________________ a new job. He started working ________________ ________________. He really likes his new job. He ________________ his parents ________________ to tell them about it.

Exercise 17 Scary Story.

Use the verbs in parentheses to fill in the blanks. Use past continuous time.

I ________________ (sit) in the dark living room. My heart ________________, (race) and a voice started to talk. "I ________________ (pass) your house, and I noticed the light. I ________________ (feel) tired, so I decided to stop." The voice ________________ (come) near to me, so I reached for the light. I ________________ (reach) for the light, and something cold touched my arm. I opened my eyes, and my puppy ________________ (lick) my hand.

Unit 8: Past Time with Irregular Verbs

WE WENT ON A FISHING TRIP.

8.1 Simple Past Time with Irregular Verbs

The most common verbs in English are irregular. You already know *be, have,* and *do.* They do not use *-ed* to make past time.

▶ **Some verbs do not change: put, cost, cut, hit, shut, hurt. (Note: All of these end in *t*, but all verbs with final *t* are not irregular.)**

Example Sentences in Context:

Yesterday I hit the door, and it shut on my hand. I cut it rather badly. I went to the hospital. The doctor put a bandage on it. It cost $45.00. That hurt even more.

▶ **Some verbs change vowel sounds. Here are some common ones:**

become: became	begin: began	bite: bit	blow: blew	break: broke
choose: chose	come: came	draw: drew	drink: drank	drive: drove
eat: ate	fall: fell	feed: fed	find: found	fly: flew
fight: fought	get: got	give: gave	grow: grew	hang: hung
hide: hid	hold: held	know: knew	meet: met	read: read
ride: rode	ring: rang	run: ran	see: saw	shake: shook
sing: sang	sit: sat	speak: spoke	steal: stole	swim: swam
take: took	tear: tore	throw: threw	wake: woke	wear: wore
win: won	write: wrote			

Example Sentences in Context:

I began my trip in Springfield. I drove to the airport, and I flew to New York. I met my brother there. We saw some of the sights of New York. We took a boat to the Statue of Liberty. We ate a nice dinner. We spoke for hours, forgot about time, and became friends again.

▶ **Some irregular verbs have a *t* (or *d*) ending with or without a vowel change:**

bend: bent	buy: bought	fight: fought	bring: brought	catch: caught
hear: heard	build: built	feel: felt	keep: kept	leave: left
lend: lent	teach: taught	lose: lost	think: thought	pay: paid
tell: told	say: said	sell: sold	send: sent	sleep: slept
spend: spent				

Example Sentences in Context:

I slept late this morning. I heard my alarm clock, but I kept shutting it off. I left the house just a few minutes late, and I caught the last bus to school. I felt awful. I spent too much time running. That taught me a lesson. I paid dearly for just ten minutes of sleep.

▶ **Some verbs are irregular and different from all others.**

You already know *be* (is, am, are, was, were); *have* (has, had); and *do* (does, did).

Other important ones are these:

go: went make: made
stand: stood understand: understood

In New York I went to the Statue of Liberty on a boat. I stood on the deck. Then I understood the symbol of freedom. It made me cry.

Exercise 1 The Magic Show.

Use the verbs in parentheses in the simple past tense.

Jerry: We ________ a magic show at school today, Mom. (have)

Emily: Tell me about it.

Jerry: Well, this guy ________ a woman in a long box. (put) Her head and feet were sticking out. Then he ________ out a big saw. (take) He ________ her in half. (cut) He moved boxes, and we ________ two separate ones— one with a head and one with two feet. (see)

Emily: Then what?

Jerry: Then he ________ the two boxes together. (put) He ________ some magic words. (say) He ________ her to get out of the box. (tell) She ________ up and ________ to sing. (get, begin)

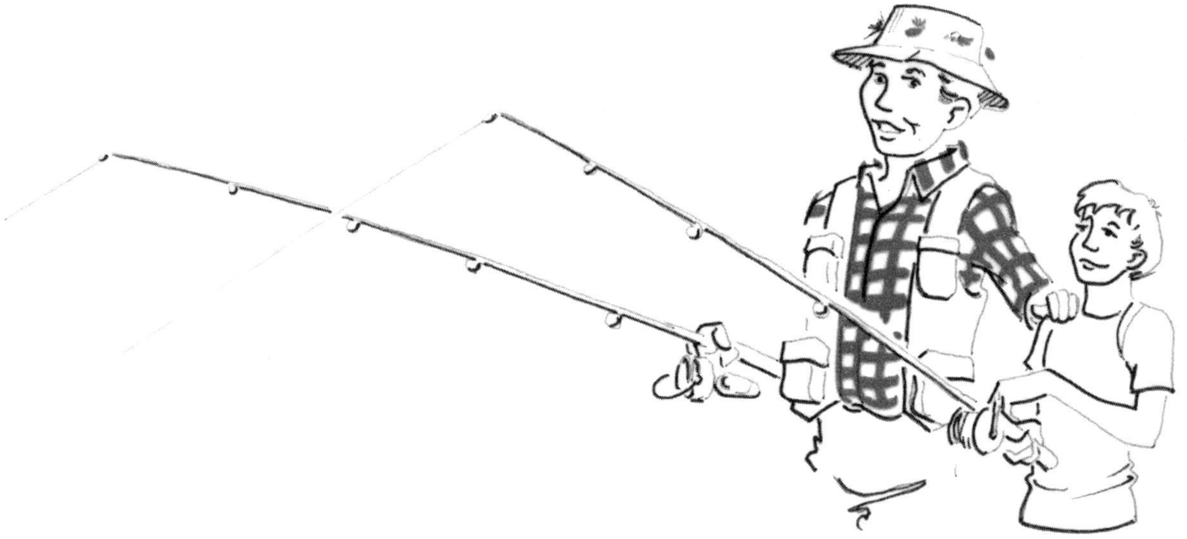

Exercise 2 The Fishing Trip.

Use the verb in parentheses to complete each of the sentences.

George and Jerry Smith ________________ (go) on a fishing trip. They ________________ (buy) some fishing poles and bait at the store. They ________________ (drive) to Lake Marshall. They ________________ (spend) three days at the lake. They ________________ (take) camping gear with them.

The first day, they ________________ (wake up) early, but they ________________ (catch) no fish at all. They ________________ (ride) into town and ________________ (buy) hot dogs. They ________________ (build) a camp fire anyway, and they ________________ (eat) well. Their luck ________________ (be) better in the morning. A big fish ________________ (bite) Jerry's bait, and it ________________ (fight) really hard. The pole ________________ (bend) and almost ________________ (break). Jerry almost ________________ (fall) out of the boat. Jerry ________________ (draw) the fish in and ________________ (get) it in the net. Jerry ________________ (hold) up the big fish, and his dad ________________ (take) the photograph.

George and Jerry ________________ (eat) that fish. It ________________ (be) delicious. The last day was stormy. The wind ________________ (blow), and clouds ________________ (hang) dark in the sky. The fish really ________________ (begin) to bite. The Smiths ________________ (sit) in their boat and pulled in the fish. They ________________ (leave) Lake Marshall with 20 fish, and the happy fishermen ________________ (sing) all the way home.

Exercise 3 The Garcia's House.

Use the verbs in parentheses to complete the sentences.

Tony, John, Andy, Rosa, Tommy, and Gloria were fixing their new house. Gloria ________________ (choose) a light brown paint, and she ________________ (begin) to paint. John ________________ (bring) some wood for the porch. He ________________ (build) some steps too. Tony ________________ (come) home from his office early. He ________________ (give) John some help. Andy ________________ (know) how to use the electric saw, so he ________________ (do) the cutting. Rosa helped too. She ________________ (find) the tools for them. Tommy ________________ (run) around helping everyone.

Exercise 4 What Did I Do? Mini-Contexts.

Complete these contexts with the verbs in parentheses.

1. Two nights ago, I ________ (lose) my keys. I ________ (forget) them somewhere. I ________ (become) angry and ________ (throw) my bag down. My keys ________ (fall) out. That ________ (make) me really mad!
2. I ________ (feel) bad. I ________ (forget) to feed my bird. I opened his cage, and I ________ (feed) him, but he ________ (fly) away.

3. Last night I ________ (read) a book in bed. I ________ (fall) asleep, and I ________ (sleep) all night with the light on. I ________ (wake up), and I ________ (tear) a page in my book.
4. I ________ (pay) ten dollars to mail a package to my sister. I ________ (send) it two weeks ago. It ________ (cost) too much, and then the gift in the box ________ (break). That lesson ________ (cost) me a lot.
5. As children, we played a lot. We ________ (swim) in the lake. We ________ (hide) in the woods. We ________ (tell) ghost stories. We ________ (get) old clothes as costumes, and we ________ (wear) them. We even ________ (write) our own shows. And then we all ________ (grow) up, and I ________ (forget) how to have fun.
6. We ________ (go) to a restaurant last night. We ________ (have) some good food. I ________ (eat) too much. I ________ (drink) too much coffee, and I stayed awake for hours.
7. I ________ (lend) a library book to a friend. She ________ (take) the book back to the library. They ________ (lose) it or someone ________ (steal) it. They don't have it, and I have a bill for $20.00.
8. I really ________ (hurt) myself yesterday. I ________ (fall) down the steps, and I ________ (hit) my head. I ________ (cut) it too. I ________ (go) to the doctor, and she ________ (put) on a bandage. The accident ________ (shake) me up.
9. Tom ________ (sell) his house last week. The new owner ________ (pay) over $100,000 for it. Tom ________ (keep) it up so well, and he ________ (take) good care of it. Tom and the new owner ________ (meet) at the house. They ________ (stand) and talked a while. Then Tom ________ (give) him the keys, turned around, walked out, and ________ (shut) the door.
10. My dad ________ (teach) me how to play sports. He always ________ (go) to our games. He always cheered. One year, we ________ (lose) ten games in a row, but Dad ________ (think) that we were great anyway. We ________ (win) our last game that season, and that ________ (make) Dad really happy.
11. Someone ________ (ring) our doorbell. I ________ (hear) someone on the porch. My dad ________ (go) to the door. He ________ (speak) with the person.
12. My teacher ________ (be) strict. He ________ (tell) us all his rules. We ________ (go) to school on time. We ________ (sit) up straight. We ________ (put) our feet flat on the floor, we ________ (do) our school work. He ________ (drive) us crazy, but we loved him. He really ________ (understand) us.

Example Sentences in Context:

Jane: It was cold last night. Did you feel cold?

Kate: Yes, I did. I felt cold enough for two blankets.

Jane: Did you put two blankets on your bed?

Kate: No, I put on two more blankets. I had four.

Do/Did	Subject	Verb	Rest of Sentence
Did	you	feel	cold?
Did	you	put	two blankets on your bed?

Grammar Note: The irregular verb follows the same pattern as regular verbs in questions.

Exercise 5 The Baby Bird.

Use the verb in parentheses to complete each sentence. Make only necessary changes.

Rosa: I ________ (find) a baby bird yesterday.

Mother: How ________ (do) it ________ (fall) out of the nest?

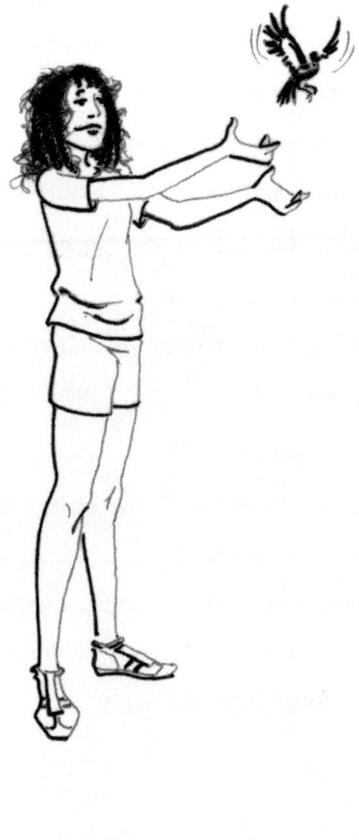

Rosa: The wind ________ (blow) the nest out of the tree. The branch ________ (break). We ________ (hear) the little bird, and we picked it up.

Mother: ________ (do) you ________ (hold) it?

Rosa: Yes, I did. It was so scared.

Mother: ________ (do) you ________ (feed) it?

Rosa: Yes, we tried. I ________ (feed) it some seeds.

Mother: ________ (do) it ________ (eat)?

Rosa: It ________ (eat) a little. And then . . .

Mother: ________ (do) the bird ________ (fly) away?

Rosa: No, it didn't. We ________ (take) it back to the same tree. We ________ (put) the nest on another branch. Then we ________ (hide) in the bushes.

Mother: ________ (do) the mother bird ________ (came) back?

Rosa: I don't know.

Exercise 6 Answer My Questions, Please.

Use the blanks to answer these questions.

1. Did you hang up your coat? Yes, ________________
2. Did you go to the store? Yes, ________________
3. Did you get milk and cheese? Yes, ________________
4. Did you bring in the dog? Yes, ________________
5. Did you take your medicine? Yes, ________________
6. Did you make your bed? Yes, ________________
7. Did you pay the newspaper boy? Yes, ________________
8. Did you wake up your Dad? Yes, ________________
9. Did you speak to the letter carrier? Yes, ________________
10. Did you shut the garage door? Yes, ________________
11. Did you understand that question? Yes, ________________
12. Did you begin your homework? Yes, ________________
13. Did you buy some bread? Yes, ________________
14. Did you forget anything? Yes, ________________
15. Do you know that I love you? Yes, ________________

Example Sentences in Context:

John *got* an A in biology. He *didn't cut* class. He *didn't forget* my homework. He *didn't sleep* during lectures. He *didn't lose* his notes. He *knew* all the answers on the test. He *did* well, *didn't* he?

Subject	DIDN'T	Verb	Rest of Sentence
He	didn't	get	an A in Biology.
He	didn't	cut	class.
He	didn't	sleep	during lectures.
He	didn't	lose	his notes.

Exercise 7 Jerry's Baseball Game.

Use the clue words in parentheses to complete the story.

Jerry had a bad day on the baseball field. He ________n't ________ (hit) the ball once. He ________n't ________ (steal) any bases. He ________n't ________ (catch) two high balls. He ________n't ________ (run) fast enough. And then he ________ (tear) his uniform. The coach ________n't ________ (get) mad. He ________ (say), "Everyone has a bad day now and then. Don't lose hope." Then Jerry ________n't ________ (feel) so bad. The coach ________ (understand) him. He ________ (leave) the game a little happier.

Exercise 8 Sam's Busy Week.

Use the underlined verb to finish the sentences.

Sam had a great day yesterday. He didn't drive to Ned's Sausage Shop today, but ________ yesterday. Sam didn't sell any meat today, but he ________ a lot yesterday. Today he didn't see any customers, but he ________ many yesterday. Sam didn't wear a clean uniform today, but he ________ one yesterday. Sam didn't have lunch at Mama Louisa's today, and he didn't ________ any lunch today. Sam is at home, and he is sick.

8.4 Simple Past Time with Adverbs

Example Sentences in Context:

Years ago no one *ever chose* young Ed Clark to be on a team. He *was always hurt* by other children. He *seldom said* anything. He *often told* his mother about it. He *usually spent* his free time alone in his room.

Then his dad helped him, and he made a change. They *frequently threw* a football to each other. They *often rode* their bikes together. They *sometimes ran* five miles. Ed got better in sports. Now he *rarely sits* around.

Subject	BE	Adverb of Frequency	Non-BE Verb	Rest of Sentence
No one	—	ever	chose	young Ed Clark.
He	was	always	hurt.	
He	—	seldom	said	anything.
He	—	often	told	his mother.
He	—	usually	spent	his free time alone.
They	—	frequently	threw	a football to each other.

Exercise 9 John and Andy Talk About College.

Complete the sentences using the words in parentheses.

Andy: How did you do so well last semester, John? You got all A's.

John: Well, ________________. (I/study/always) ________________. (usually/go to bed/I/early)________________. (I/frequently/early/get up/to study) ________________. (be late/I/never) ________________. (takes notes/always/I)

Andy: Didn't you ever have any fun at all?

John: Sure. ____________. (sometimes/take a girl/to the library/to study/I) ____________. (seldom/go on a real date/I)

Andy: ____________. (didn't go out/you/often enough/in my opinion)

Exercise 10 Andy's Broken Arm.

Use these words to make past time sentences.

1. break/arm/Andy/last year,/but it is fine now

   ____

2. take care of it/he/every day

   ____

3. it/so/get better

   ____

4. wear/for the first three weeks/always/he/his sling

   ____

5. rarely/he/get his cast wet

   ____

6. he/seldom/try to use his hand

   ____

7. sometimes/he/go swimming

   ____

8. his exercises/do/usually/he

   ____

9. disobey/he/the doctor/never

   ____

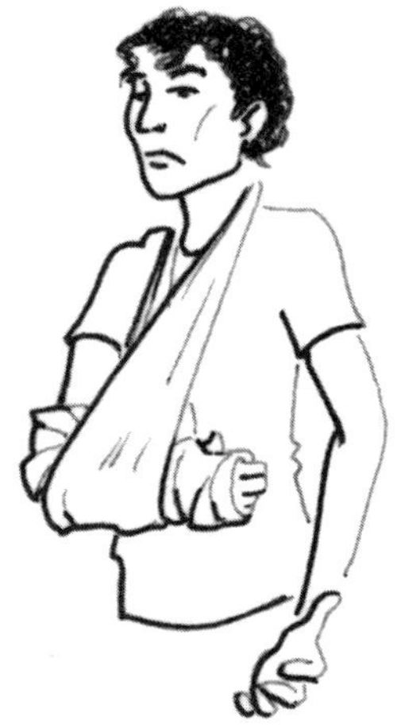

10. often/he/put his arm up on pillows

____

11. take time to exercise/he frequently

____

12. always/he/on time/be/for physical therapy

____

8.5 Comparison of Present Time and Past Time Then and Now

Example Sentences in Context:

I *was* a fat child, but I'*m* thin now. I *had* a lot of friends then, and I *have* many friends now. I *swam* a lot as a child, and I still *do*. I *wrote* stories in grade school, but now I *write* books. I *was always writing* something then, and today I *am writing* a novel. I *was writing* my first book in fifth grade. Mr. Snow *became* my teacher then. He *taught* me a lot about writing. I still *remember* him today.

Grammar Note: Use the simple times (present and past) to talk about happenings of limited duration or past memories. The verb BE is different: *I was being happy* is *not* good English, *I was having + a noun* is also unusual. Use the continuous times (present and past) to talk about happenings of long duration. (They last a long time and perhaps still continue.) It takes a long time to write a book, for example. The writer starts and then writes over a long period. The continuous tense shows this relationship.

Use one simple and one continous time to show a comparison: *I was writing* a book over a period of six months. I *got sick*. The *getting sick* was only one moment. The writing took six months.

For a memory of the past, use simple past tense. To compare the simple tenses with continuous tenses, look at these examples.

Present Time:

I open my window. [I do it every day. It is my habit.]

I am opening my window. [*Now* I am doing it.]

She studies math with Kate. [They always study together.]

She is studying math with Kate. [That's what she and Kate are doing now.]

He watches TV. [He does it a lot. He is often in front of the TV set.]

He is watching TV. [What's he doing now? Oh, he's watching TV.]

Past Time:

We opened the package. [It happened once, and then it was finished.]

We were opening the package. [and something else happened at the same time.]

I studied math. [I was a college student, but I'm not anymore.]

I once studied math. [What did I do last night? I studied math.]

I was studying math. [but something stopped me . . . the telephone rang or someone came in to talk to me.]

We watched TV. [last night, for a limited time.]

We were watching TV. [When the storm began, the telephone rang, or something else happened to stop us.]

Spelling Note: Spelling the ***-ing*** form of the verb. (See 5.2) There are rules for adding ***-ed*** to verbs, and there are similar rules for adding ***-ing***.

► **Some verbs end in two vowels and a consonant:**

break eat read feel rain hear meet speak wear keep

► **Some verbs end in two or three consonants:**

bring build catch watch fight hold sing stand understand

► **Some verbs end in *-w*, *-x*, and *-y*:**

blow fix mix try buy

For all of these verbs, add only *-ing*:

breaking	bringing	blowing
eating	building	fixing
reading	catching	mixing
feeling	watching	trying
raining	fighting	buying

► **Some verbs end in *-e*:**

shave write bite drive give have take make

For these verbs, drop the *e*, and then add *-ing:*

shaving biting giving taking
writing driving having making

► **Some verbs end in one vowel and one consonant:**

get put cut win run

For these verbs, add a second consonant of the same kind. Then add *-ing:*

get + t + ing = getting
win + n + ing = winning
putting cutting running

Exercise 11 Doing It Now. Mini-Contexts.

Change the verb in the parentheses to an -ing *form. Add an appropriate form of* BE.

1. We ________________ (sail) along on Golden Bay.
   People ________________ (sing) some old songs.
2. The Jacksons ________________ (build) a new house.
   They ________________ (buy) a large lot for the house.
   The workmen ________________ (mix) concrete for the basement.
3. Sara ________________ (cook) supper.
   She ________________ (fix) steak and vegetables.
   She ________________ (cut) the carrots.
   She ________________ also ________________ (peel) some potatoes.
   She ________________ (bake) a cake for dessert.
4. This morning, Kate ________________ (try) to get to school on time.
   She ________________ (get) ready.
   She ________________ (take) a shower.
   She ________________ (put) on her makeup.
   She ________________ (fix) her hair.
   Her mother ________________ (watch) her.

5. Ricky ________________ (play) in the yard now.
   He ________________ (ride) his new tricycle.
   He ________________ (sing) too.

6. Allison ________________ (clean) her room now.
   She ________________ (sweep) the floor.
   She ________________ (stand) on the chair to clean the shelves.
   She ________________ (dust) the furniture.

7. Pam is at the hairdresser's.
   Max ________________ (wash) her hair.
   He ________________ (cut) it too.
   He ________________ (add) some color.
   He ________________ (blow) her hair to dry it.
   He ________________ (set) it.
   He ________________ (comb) it out.

8. Ed ________________ (drive) on the highway last week.
   He didn't know it, but he ________________ (run) out of gas.
   He ________________ (wait) for someone to help him, but no one stopped.
   He ________________ (see) the other cars go by, and he ________________ (get) angry. Then he walked to a phone booth and called home.

Exercise 12 This Was Happening, and That Happened. Mini-Contexts.

There are two sentences in each pair below. They are both in simple time. Change one to continuous time. Rewrite the two sentences. Write the continuous sentence first.

Example: **It rained. The lightning struck a house.**
It was raining, and the lightning struck a house.

1. It snowed. There was a car accident.

   ____

   The car turned around. It hit a tree.

   ____

   A man got out of the car. The police arrived.

   ____

2. The bell rang. The new student walked into the classroom.

   ____

   The teacher came in. The other students talked.

   ____

   The new student talked to the teacher. The other students started to study.

   ____

3. The mother read a book in a chair under an umbrella. Her children played in the sand.

____

The waves came higher on the beach. The children moved away from the ocean.

____

Their mother read still. The waves came up to her chair.

____

4. The sun came up. The birds sang.

____

The man walked across the field. A car drove up.

____

The man looked. A child got out of the car.

____

The child called, "Daddy, Daddy." The child ran to him.

____

5. I took a nap. Someone came into my room.

____

I woke up. Someone looked into my closet.

____

I called the police. The thief ran away.

____

6. The teacher taught the class. The bell rang.

____

Andy slept in class. The bell rang.

____

Andy woke up. The bell rang.

____

Unit 9: Nouns and Pronouns

APPLES, SUGAR, AND OTHER FOOD

9.1 Count Nouns and Non-Count Nouns

Example Sentences in Context:

Tom: Do you have any money?
Bill: About twenty-five dollars. Why?
Tom: I don't have any money, but I need some food from the grocery store.
Bill: Like what?
Tom: Bread, cheese, meat, milk, butter, and sugar.
Bill: Anything else?
Tom: Apples, oranges, bananas, some vegetables, and a pound of rice.

Grammar Note: Some of the underlined words in the example sentences have two forms: singular and plural. We call these count nouns. (Some do not have two forms. They are the non-count nouns.)

one dollar	twenty-five dollars
one apple	two apples
an orange	two oranges
one vegetable	some vegetables*

*Note: *Some* can come before count and non-count nouns. (See 9.2 on page 142.)

Exercise 1 Think of Names.

Make a list for each answer.

1. What's in your desk?
____
2. What's in your backpack?
____
3. What's in your closet? (clothes)
____
4. What's in the cupboard? (food)
____
5. What things do you use for cleaning?
____
6. What are some things with motors?
____
7. What do you like to eat?
____
8. What furniture do you have in your house?
____
9. What are some common tools?
____
10. What's in a playground?
____

Spelling Note: In your lists for these answers, you wrote many nouns. Many (or maybe all) of your words are count nouns. Most count nouns take *-s* or *-es* to make plurals. There are some rules to follow.

▶ **Some nouns end in consonant + *y*:**

cit**y** cop**y** count**ry** categ**ory**

To make a plural, we change the *y* to *i* and add *-es*:

cit**ies** cop**ies** count**ries** categor**ies**

▶ **Some common nouns for food end in consonant + *o*:**

tomat**o** potat**o**

We add *-es* to these two words:

tomat**oes** potat**oes**

▶ **Some nouns end in *-f* or *-fe*:**

life wife thief knife wolf leaf

The *-f* or *-fe* changes into *-ves* for the plural:

lives wives thieves knives wolves leaves

▶ **Some nouns end in *-s*, *-ch*, *-ss*, *-x*:**

wish watch kiss ax

Add *-es* to these words to make plurals:

wishes watches kisses axes

Add *-s* to all other regular count nouns. (Some nouns are irregular. See 9.2.)

Exercise 2 More Than One. Mini-Contexts.

Add -s *or* -es *to these nouns. Change the spelling if necessary. Complete the sentences.*

1. My two favorite ________ (vegetable) are ________ (tomato) and ________ (potato). I also like ________ (carrot) and ________ (beet).
2. Set the table for dinner. Put out five ________ (plate), ________ (cup), ________ (knife), ________ (fork), and ________ (spoon). We also need ________ (cup) for coffee and small ________ (dish) for dessert.
3. There isn't much food in the house. There are two ________ (apple), six ________ (tomato), four ________ (onion), one ________ (hot dog), and two ________ (cracker).
4. The United States has fifty ________ (state). Each state has many smaller ________ (part). In Louisiana, the ________ (county) have a different name, ________ (parish). There are several very large ________ (city) in the US.
5. In the fall, the ________ (tree) lose their ________ (leaf). The ________ (flower) die, and the ________ (bird) fly to warm places.

6. The ________ (forest) are full of ________ (animal). There are ________ (bird), ________ (bear), ________ (beaver), and ________ (chipmunk). There are some ________ (fox) and ________ (wolf) too. In the ________ (river) and ________ (stream) there are ________ (frog) and ________ (snake). On the ________ (lake), there are ________ (duck).
7. I like big ________ (city). There are ________ (museum), ________ (library), ________ (theater), and lots of ________ (store). I like to go to big baseball ________ (game) and to visit new ________ (place). Unfortunately, in big ________ (city), there are also lots of ________ (car) and lots of noise. There are also bad people — like ________ (thief).
8. It's fun to watch people at ________ (airport). They carry lots of ________ (thing). They say hello and goodbye with ________ (hug) and ________ (kiss). They sit and read ________ (novel) and ________ (newspaper), and they look bored.

9.2 Some and Any

Count nouns can use numbers. *One, a,* or *an* can come before a single count noun.
Use *an* before a vowel or vowel sound at the beginning of a word: an apple, an orange, an animal, an hour, an egg.
Plural count nouns do not use *a* or *an*. (*A* and *an* mean *one*.)

Examples:

We have a lot of pets: two dogs, an old cat, and some tropical fish.

In this sentence the number of pets is clear, exact, except for the fish. *Some fish* is an indefinite number. (Perhaps we have ten fish or maybe fifteen. I'm not sure.)

REMEMBER: you can use *some* and *any* with both plural count nouns and non-count nouns.

Both *some* and *any* are used in questions, with or without *not*:

a. Do you have some pets?
b. Don't you have some pets?
c. Do you have any pets?
d. Don't you have any pets?

Questions *a* and *b* = (I think) you have pets, so I'm asking this way.
Questions *c* and *d* = (I think) you don't have pets, but I'm asking anyway.
The short answers:

Yes, I do. or *Yes, I have some.*

No, I don't. or *No, I don't have any.*

Grammar Note: With a negative verb, use *any*:

We don't have *any birds*.

Exercise 3 Some and Any.

Answer these questions for yourself. Use numbers or number expressions.

Example: Jane: Do you have any pens with you?
Kate: Yes, I have some. I have four.

1. Do you have any pencils with you?

   ____

2. Did you bring some books to school?

   ____

3. Were there any problems with the homework?

   ____

4. Are there any tall people in your family?

   ____

5. Do you have some tools at home?

   ____

6. Do you know any people from Yugoslavia?

   ____

7. Do you have any new friends?

   ____

8. Do you read any books for fun?

   ____

Summary of measure words and phrases:
some (a little, not many, not much)
any (*not* + some)
a pound of (a weighted amount; also a *kilo*, an *ounce*, a *ton*)
a gallon of (a liquid; also a *liter*, a *pint*, a *quart*, a *cup*)

a piece of (a normal section; also a *slice*, a *head*, a *bunch*, a *bottle*)
a pair of (things with two parts — gloves, scissors, pants, stockings)

There are many foods that are non-count nouns:

food	milk	sugar	cheese	pepper	soup
meat	flour	oil	salt	rice	coffee
fruit	bread	water	fish	honey	tea
salad	dessert	lettuce	cabbage		

Types of meat are also non-count nouns:

beef chicken lamb mutton pork ham bacon

Grammar Note: Count and non-count nouns are different in two ways:

a. non-count nouns do not have an *-s* form.
b. they frequently (but not always) need a "measure word or phrase."

Count nouns take numbers, and non-count nouns are amounts. *Some* and *any* with non-count nouns mean an indefinite amount.

Exercise 4 What Did You Eat for Dinner?

Use non-count nouns in your answers.

1. I had some ________________.
2. (Ask a friend.) My friend ________________ (name) had ________________ for dinner.
3. (What foods don't you like?) I don't like ________________, so I don't eat any ________________.

You sometimes hear a food non-count noun with an *-s* on it. The meaning is usually "kinds of . . . " For example:

That restaurant has many salads. = They make many kinds of salad (green salad, fruit salad, potato salad, cooked vegetable salad. . . .)

They are famous for their breads: (white bread, French bread, rye bread, bread sticks).

Some people also drop the measure words or phrases:

"Waiter, please bring two coffees." (two cups of coffee) (This is informal English.)

Exercise 5 "What Do You Want to Order?"

Here is a menu from the Country Club Dining Room:

Country Club DINING ROOM

Today's Special

Roast Beef ... $14.95
Barbecued Chicken ... $12.95
Fresh Fish ... $12.95
Lamb ... $11.95
Fish & Chips ... $ 8.95

ALL DINNERS INCLUDE:
- *Rice, Baked Potato, or Noodles*
- *Soup or Salad*
- *Bread*
- *Spinach, Green Beans, or Carrots*
- *Dessert (Cake, Pie, Ice Cream)*
- *Coffee or Tea*

DRINKS

Coffee or Tea . . . $1.00
Soft Drinks ... $1.00
Wine (Ask to see the wine list)
By the glass (White, Red, Rose) . . . $2.50

DESSERTS

Cake, Pie, or Ice Cream . . . $2.50

Now order a dinner from the menu. Use *some*:

I want some ____

____.

Now practice ordering dinner from the menu with a classmate.

> **Grammar Note:** Some important non-count nouns are general words:
>
> (your) help (some) advice (that) information (the) news (our) health

Example Sentences:

"I need some help. Please give me some advice and some information."

"No news is good news."

Some other common non-count nouns:

money mail music homework paper weather work furniture
room stuff jewelry equipment

REMEMBER: A non-count noun always uses a singular verb. It does not use *a* or *an*.

Exercise 6 Count Nouns.

Add -s *or* -es *for each count noun. Use a number or measure word in the blank before a noun or pronoun. Put a dash in a blank after a non-count noun.*

Jack and Bill are new roommates at the dorm at Taylor College. They are talking about their room and all their things. They are unpacking.

Jack: Do you have ________ book____?

Bill: Not ________. I have only ________ box____. How about you? How ________ book____ do you have?

Jack: I have ________ bookcase____ full, but I left ________ at home. I have ________ clock radio, ________ tape player, and ________ tape____.

Bill: Oh yeah? What kind of music____ do you like?

Jack: Oh, all kind____ — classical, jazz, pop, rock, country western.

Bill: Great. I have ________ tape____ too. Hey, do you have ________ furniture?

Jack: I have ________ chair____ and ________ lamp____. Do we have ________ place____ for them?

Bill: Sure — we'll find ________ room for everything.

Jack: Here's ________ coffeemaker and ________ coffee mug____.

Bill: Terrific! Let's have ________ coffee.

Jack: I'll make ________, but I don't have ________ sugar____ or ________ milk____.

Bill: That's OK. I don't need ________ sugar____ or ________ milk. I like my coffee black.

Exercise 7 What Do You See? Mini-Contexts.

Use a *or* an *with count nouns and measure words and phrases for non-count nouns.*

1. Look around your room. What do your see?

____

____

2. What kind of furniture do you see in your living room?

I see a ________________________________

____.

3. What do you see at the bookstore?

I see a ________________________________

____.

4. What do you see at the library?

I see a ________________________________

____.

5. What do you see in a supermarket?

I see a ________________________________

____.

Exercise 8 An Hour, A Day. Mini-Contexts.

Use a *or* an *before each noun. Use* an *before a vowel sound.*

1. Sara went to the supermarket to do the shopping. She wanted to make ________ fruit salad for dinner, so she bought ________ apple, ________ orange, ________ banana, ________ melon, and ________ pineapple. She bought some other foods too: ________ loaf of bread, ________ pound of butter, ________ beef roast, ________ onion, ________ package of beans, and ________ bag of potatoes.
2. At the zoo, we saw some interesting animals. There was ________ elephant, ________ giraffe, ________ dozen monkeys, ________ ostrich, ________ emu, and ________ enormous turtle.
3. The Royal Table Restaurant menu was a list of interesting foods. They had ________ creamed fish dish, ________ special seafood salad, and ________ fruit soup.
4. The library in Springfield is full of books and many other things. They have ________ video theater, ________ children's book corner, ________ adult magazine center, and ________ rent-a-poster section. Mrs. Joanne Collins, the librarian, believes that ________ library is ________ center of community activity.

Exercise 9 Countable or Not? Mini-Contexts.

Read these sentences carefully. Are the nouns countable in these sentences? Write a *(or* an*) in the blank for each singular count noun. Write* — *(for no article),* some*, or* any*, for non-count pronouns or plural count nouns.*

1. Amy made lunches for herself and the other Walker children. In each lunch box, she put ________ orange, ________ egg salad sandwich, ________ can of juice, and ________ raw vegetables. Sara, her mother, is ________ administrator at the hospital. She knows the importance of good health and good food.
2. At Taylor College, the new students need ________ information about new classes. So they go to see ________ faculty advisor. From ________ advisor they get ________ information about classes and ________ advice about schedules and requirements. ________ good advisor gives ________ new student ________ help at the start of ________ college work.
3. To ________ Japanese students, ________ American house is full of ________ furniture. Even ________ dormitory room is full. Each student gets ________ desk, ________ chair, ________ chest of drawers, ________ bed, and ________ closet. ________ Japanese rooms have only ________ tables and boxes and ________ sleeping mat for ________ furniture.
4. John Garcia is ________ student at Taylor College. He goes to the library every day to study. He has ________ homework for all of this classes. John wants to be ________ dentist.
5. I need ________ supplies for school: ________ paper, ________ pencils, ________ notebooks, and ________ new dictionary. My mother gave me ________ money to buy these things, but I need to get ________ job too. A student needs to earn ________ money of his own.

6. In the summer, it's often hot, but I love the cool air of October. I really love ________ cool weather.

7. Jerry: Mom, you have ________ mail. The letter carrier just left it.
   Emily: What is it, Jerry?
   Jerry: There's ________ letter from Grandma, ________ bills, and ________ advertisement from Ruby's Department Store.
   Emily: Let me read the letter first. Perhaps there's ________ news about my sister's baby.

Exercise 10 A Cup of Tea. Mini-Contexts.

Each of these nouns is a non-count noun. Use a "measure" expression to complete the sentences. Here are some measure expressions.

a lot of	a spoonful of	a cup of
a pound of	a glass of	a gallon of
a dish of	a bowl of	a quart of
a slice of	a piece of	a serving of

NOTE: You can say *two* cups of . . . . *A lot of* works the same way, but it means *many.*

1. To make a sandwich, you need two ________ bread, ________ cheese, ________ mayonnaise, ________ tomato, and ________ lettuce.
2. For breakfast I usually have ________ orange juice, ________ milk, ________ toast, an egg, and ________ cereal.
3. At a restaurant, you get ________ roast beef, ________ salad, ________ tomato juice, and ________ vegetables.
4. At the gas station, Tony bought ten ________ gasoline and ________ oil for his car.
5. The real estate agent showed the Garcias ________ land by the lake. They bought it for a summer home.
6. Sara Walker gave Gary ________ medicine for his cold. Then she gave him ________ hot tea and ________ orange juice.
7. Everyone wanted a different dessert. Emily had ________ cake, and George ordered ________ pie. Jerry had ________ ice cream, and Peggy had ________ berries with cream.
8. At the hardware store, Ed bought a new hammer, ________ nails, and ________ cleaning liquid.

9.3 A Lot of, a Few, a Little, Much, and Many

There are some other common measure words. With both count and non-count nouns, use *a lot of.* With count nouns, use *many.* With non-count nouns, use *much.* The opposite of *many* is a *few.* The opposite of *much* is *a little.*

Example Sentences in Context:

I have *a lot of* money, but just *a little* with me. I don't carry *much* money. It's not a good idea.

I know *a lot of* people, but just *a few* are really good friends. A person can't have *many* friends.

Count Nouns	Non-Count Nouns
a lot of friends	a lot of money
a few friends	a little money
many friends	much money

Exercise 11 A Lot of People.

Use the count noun measures or the non-count measure words to complete the following mini-contexts.

1. Springfield has ________________ stores, but there isn't ________________ traffic on the roads.

2. ________________ young people go to Taylor College. There are ________________ students from out of town there, too. The students of Taylor College give Springfield business. ________________ people from Springfield work at Taylor College.

3. ________________ students from all over the world want to study abroad. ________________ are able to do so. ________________ come to the United States to study. ________________ want to become engineers. ________________ want to study business. ________________ study foreign languages.

4. Do you know how to make a fruit salad? You cut up ________________ fruit, and then you add ________________ orange juice or ________________ mayonnaise. ________________ people add ________________ raisins or ________________ dates.

5. Sara Walker is a busy woman, so she uses her time well. She doesn't have ________________ time for cooking, so she buys ________________ frozen vegetables. She doesn't want her family to eat ________________ junk food, so she buys ________________ fruits, too. Everyone (Jason, Amy, Allison, and Gary) helps with the meals. Gary doesn't do ________ cooking yet, but he is learning.

6. Dr. Shirley Cook sees ________________ patients. She is a children's doctor, so she treats ________________ broken arms, cuts and bruises, and children's diseases. Most cuts need only ________________ stitches. Most children are just frightened, but Dr. Cook gives them ________________ gentle care. Then they feel a lot better.

Example Sentences in Context:

Sara and Jason decided to take their *children* to the zoo in the city. There were many *people* there. Two *women* were feeding the monkeys, and two *men* were cleaning the elephant yard.

Gary watched closely. He saw the big *teeth* of the tiger, the big *feet* of the elephant, and the long pink tails of the white *mice*. At the end of the day, they all went to see the *fish* in the aquarium.

Note: Most count nouns use the *-s/-es* plural, but some very common ones do not.

child — children	foot — feet	fish — fish
man — men	tooth — teeth	deer — deer
woman — women	mouse — mice	sheep — sheep

Exercise 12 Two, Not Just One.

Make the underlined word a plural. Rewrite the sentence. Make all necessary changes.

1. There is a beautiful deer in the zoo. It is from China. There is a sheep from Australia too.

   ____

   ____

2. A child needs to learn how to act like a man or a woman.

   ____

   ____

3. Coach O'Brien was talking to a child. He said, "Are you a man or a mouse?" The little person said, "A mouse, I think. I'm not a man, so I must be a mouse."

   ____

   ____

   ____

4. I'm having a bad day. My foot hurts, and my tooth hurts. I want to go back to bed.

   ____

   ____

5. The person in the boat caught a fish. The man was very happy about it.

   ____

   ____

6. There are animals in the barn. There is a mouse there, and there is a sheep too.

   ____

   ____

9.5 Possessive Nouns *(Regular and Irregular)*

Example Sentences in Context:

Ann *Clark's* family works together well. Her *mother's* job as a lawyer is hard, and her *father's* work as a professor is too. So everyone helps with the work around the house. The *parents'* job is to fix the meals. The laundry is *Ann's* job. Keeping the house clean and doing the dishes is *everyone's* job.

Noun + 's	Noun
Ann Clark's	family
her mother's	job
her father's	work
the parents'	house
everyone's	friend

Grammar Note: To show possession (that one person owns something), we use an apostrophe (') and an *s* after the owner noun (my mother's house).

For a plural noun that ends in *-s* (like *parents*), we use just an apostrophe (my parents' house).

Example Sentences in Context:

Shopping malls are an important part of *people's* lives today. Everything is there under one roof. For example, a mall is likely to have a couple of department stores, a *children's* shop, and *men*'s store, and several *women's* dress shops.

Grammar Note: The irregular plural nouns like *people* and *children* act just like other nouns. Add the (*'s*) to a noun without an *s* at the end. Add just an (*'*) to a noun with an *s* at the end.

Practice Add (*'s*) or (*'*) to the first noun to show possession.

A.
1. Springfield____ mall
2. Radio Hut____ advertisement
3. Ruby____ Department Store
4. L and J Men____ Store
5. Pete____ Pizza
6. Martin____ Department Store
7. Buck____ Car Repair
8. Ned____ Sausage Shop
9. Flanagan____ Meats
10. Big Joe____ Steak House
11. Conway____ Ice Cream
12. Wen Po____ Chinese Kitchen
13. Mama Luisa____ Italian Restaurant
14. Dr. Garcia____ office
15. a women____ dress shop
16. a children____ toystore
17. Wilson____ Shoes
18. everyone____ favorite place
19. stores____ names
20. O'Hara____ Hardware

B.
1. the Walkers____ trip to the zoo
2. the elephants____ area
3. the monkeys____ bananas
4. the kangaroos____ babies
5. the giraffe____ long neck
6. the lion____ big mouth
7. the polar bears____ pool
8. the gorilla____ fur
9. the zebra____ stripes
10. the anteaters____ long noses
11. the panda____ paws
12. the deers____ antlers
13. the tiger____ teeth
14. the squirrels____ tails
15. the zoo____ animals
16. the sharks____ tank
17. the turtles____ shells
18. the birds____ cage
19. the people____ map
20. the zookeepers____ truck

Exercise 13 Mrs. Watson and the Third Grade.

Add ('s) or (') to show possession. Write a — in a blank if no ('s) or (') is necessary.

1. Mrs. Watson____ third grade class is putting on a play for their school on Wednesday morning.
2. They have only two days____ to get ready.
3. Tommy____ mother is making him a costume. He needs a king____ crown and a long robe.

4. Mary is the queen, so her_____ mother is making her a crown too. Mary_____ gown is long and silky.
5. The other children_____ are soldiers, townspeople, and farmers.
6. The farmers_____ costumes are blue jeans, straw hats, and plaid shirts.
7. The soldiers_____ wear dark pants, green T-shirts, and tall hats with feathers.
8. The townspeople_____ costumes are ordinary clothes.
9. The children_____ parents are all helping.
10. Judy_____ dad is fixing the lights. Todd_____ dad is building the set.
11. Stacey_____ mother is painting scenery. Sometimes Billy_____ mother and Rachel _____ dad paint too.
12. Joshua_____ mother is playing the piano for the play.

Exercise 14 Putting It All Together.

Add -s *or* -es *for each count noun. Use a number or measure word in the blank before a noun or pronoun. Put an X in a blank if nothing goes in it. Show possession if necessary.*

Someone broke into Shirley Cook's house last night. Tim Hall, a police officer, is asking questions:

Tim: What did they take?

Shirley: Well, they took ________ money_____—about two hundred dollar_____. And my television set_____, the VCR, ________ box of video tape_____. My mother_____ dish_____ and her silver_____ are also missing.

Tim: What about your jewelry_____? Did they take ________ jewelry_____?

Shirley: Yes, they took it all. It was in two box____, and they are both missing.

Tim: What was in them?

Shirley: Oh, ________ ring____, ________ necklace____, ________ earring ____, and ________ old coin____. And they also took ________ really funny thing____.

Tim: Like what?

Shirley: Well, like food____. They took two frozen pizza____, ________ chocolate cake____, ________ soda, and ________ potato chip____.

Tim: It sounds like a party to me.

Unit 10: Modals and Other Special Verbs

WE CAN DO IT!

10.1 Modals to Show Preference

Example Sentences in Context:

Ed: Where *would* you *like to* go for vacation?

Pam: I *like to* swim. How about the beach?

Ed: Do you *want to* go to Florida?

Pam: That's OK, but how about you? What *would* you *like to* do?

Ed: Well, let me think. . . . I *need to* check some manuscripts at the Library of Congress in Washington. *Would* you *like to* go to Washington?

Pam: That sounds fine. There are beaches near there. Ann *would like* that, too. She *likes to* swim, shop, and go to libraries and museums.

(Question Word Order)	Subject	Modal	Verb	Rest of Sentence
Where would	you	like to	go	for vacation?
	I	like to	swim.	
Do	you	want to	go	to Florida?
	I	need to	check	some manuscripts.
	She	likes to	swim.	

Note: Use all of these modals to mean "I want to," but there are some differences:

I need to = I want to do it, and someone else wants me to do it, too.
I need to = I don't want to, but someone else wants me to do it.

I need to means *Maybe I want to do it, and maybe I don't. Someone or something else wants me to do it. It is necessary for me to do it.*

I like to = I enjoy it.
I would like to = I want to do it. Is it OK with you?

Note: Three of these modals can be used with another noun or pronoun: I want you to go there. I would like you to go there. I need you to help me.

Exercise 1 Please Help Me.

Complete the sentences. Use the clue words in parentheses.

Pam: Ann, help me pack. ________________. (I/finish/need to)

Ann: OK, Mom. ________________? (what/you/me/do/would like to)

Pam: ________________. (I/take/two blouses/need to) ________________ (you/choose/them/want to/for me)

Ann: OK. ________________? (you/take/a couple of suits/want to)

Pam: Yes, the navy blue one and the grey one.

Ann: Don't ________________? (you/pack/some dresses/want to)

Pam: Good idea. I _______________. (have with me/three dresses/would like to)

Ann: How are these three?

Pam: They are fine. But maybe I _______________. (take/one more/need to) And Ann, thanks. _______________ now? (you/pack/need to/for yourself)

Ann: Yes, I _______________ now. (start/would like to)

Exercise 2 What Would You Like? Mini-Contexts.

Use the elements in parentheses to complete the sentences.

1. (Ed is on the phone. He is calling Trans World Airlines, TWA.)

   Ed: I _______________ information on flights to Washington. (have/would like)

   TWA: When _______________ go? (you/would like to)

   Ed: Well, we _______________ in Washington on the twenty-first. (be/need to) We _______________ on an early flight, if possible. (go/would like to)

   TWA: There's a flight at ten A.M. _______________ a reservation? (you/make/want to)

   Ed: Yes, I _______________ three seats. (would like to/reserve)

2. (At Ruby's Department Store)

   Peggy: Tomorrow is our dad's birthday. We _______________. (get/for him/something special/would like to)

Clerk: How much ________? (you/spend/want to)

Jerry: We have twenty dollars, but we ________. (buy/need to/a card too)

Clerk: ________? (he/would like to/a new tie/have) Or perhaps ________? (need to/buy/some new handkerchiefs/you)

Jerry: No handkerchiefs and no ties. They are too boring. He ________. (get/would like to/something different)

Clerk: Well, does you dad ________? (fish/like to)

Jerry: Yes, . . .

Clerk: Why don't you try the sports department? There are many things for dads there.

3. (In the Sports Department at Ruby's)

Jerry: We ________ for our dad. (buy/a present/need to)

Peggy: We ________ about twenty dollars. (would like to/spend)

Jerry: We ________ him something really nice. (want to/buy)

Clerk: ________ golf? (like to/your dad/play)

Jerry: Yes.

Clerk: How about some personalized golf balls?

Peggy: Oh, he ________ golf balls with his name on them! (play with/would love to)

4. (At a restaurant at the airport)

Waiter: Do you ________ now? (order/want to)

Bill: Yes, I ________. (would like to)

Waiter:	________________ the specials for today? (you/know/want to)
Bill:	No. I ________________ quickly. (order/need to) I don't have much time. ________________ (I/steak/would like to/with a baked potato/order)
Waiter:	________________? (you/anything to drink/have/would like to)
Bill:	Yes, I ________________ your famous tropical punch. (try/want to)

NOTE: *I would like to go.* = *I'd like to go.* The *would like* becomes *'d like.*

Exercise 3 I'd Like to Go.

Change the full form of would like to *to* 'd like to.

1. I have a lot of dreams. Someday I would like to travel all over the world.
   ____
2. I would like to own a nice car. ________________________
3. I would like to have a family. ________________________
4. I would like to be able to afford a good education for my children.
   ____

(What Did She Say About Her Dreams?)

5. She would like to travel.
   ____
6. She would like to own a nice car.
   ____
7. She would like to have a family.
   ____
8. She would like to send her children to college.
   ____

Note: *I can go.* = *I have permission* and *I am able to go.*
I may go. = only permission with both present and future meaning.
I might go. = *Maybe I will go in the future.*
I could go. = *Maybe I will go.* There is a possibility.
(See 10.5)

Example Sentences in Context:

Ann: Dr. Hunter, may I talk with you this afternoon?

Dr. Hunter: Of course you can. I have office hours right after class. Can you stop by my office then?

Ann: I could, but I need to run to the bookstore. Could I come at 2:30?

Dr. Hunter: I'm not able to be there then. There's a faculty meeting at 2:30.

Ann: I could go to the bookstore later.

Dr. Hunter: Well, the faculty meeting might be over by 3:00.

Ann: That's fine. See you then.

(Question Word Order)	Subject	Modal	Verb	Rest of Sentence
May	I	—	talk	with you this afternoon?
	You	can.		
Can	you	—	stop by	then?
	I	could.		
Could	I	—	come	at 2:30?
	I	am not able to	be	there then.
	I	could	go	to the bookstore later.
	The faculty meeting	might	be over	by 3:00.

Note: Permission words: can could, may, might.
Ability words: can, could, be able to, might be able to.
Possibility words: could, might.

Exercise 4 May I? Can I?

Use the clue words to finish the sentences.

Joe: _________________ with you in the morning? (I/run/could) I'd like to get into shape.

Tom: Sure. Be ready at six o'clock.

Joe: Where do you usually run?

Tom: Well, I have three routes. We ______________ down Main Street and across the bridge. (could/run) Or we ______________ down Maple Street and around the mall. (can/go) Some days I just run around Taylor College campus. ______________ that. (We/could/do)

Joe: I ______________ ('d like to/the route around the mall/try), but ______________ (might not/I/make it)

Tom: Let's start with the Taylor College run. ______________ on a longer run after that. (go/may/I)

Joe: Thanks, Tom. That sounds great. That way I ______________ a start (can/get), and you ______________. (keep going/can)

Exercise 5 Yes, I Can. Mini-Contexts.

Use a modal expression to show preference (want to, would like to, need to, like to), *ability* (can, could, be able to), *permission* (can, could, may, might), *or possibility* (might, could).

1. Gary: Mom, ______________ go to the movies with Jerry? (permission)

   Sara: What's playing?

   Gary: We ______________ see "Space Monster." (preference)

   Sara: What times are the shows?

   Gary: We ______________ go to the 5 o'clock show. (preference) We ______________ get the one dollar rush hour tickets (ability), and Jerry's mom ______________ pick us up at 7:00 after the show. (ability)

2. (At the eye doctor's office)

   Dr. Aboud: Tommy, ______________ you see this chart? (ability)

   Tommy: Yes, I ______________. (ability)

Dr. Aboud:	I ________________ have you start reading this line. (preference)
Tommy:	E G P D A . . .
Dr. Aboud:	You ________________ need glasses. (possibility) ________________ you read this line? (ability)
Tommy:	No, I ________________. (ability)
Dr. Aboud:	Try this one.
Tommy:	I ________________n't see that line either. (ability)

3. (At the post office)

Gloria Garcia:	I ________________ mail this package. (preference)
Postmaster:	How ________________ send it? (preference)
Gloria:	I ________________ get it to New York by next Tuesday. (preference)
Postmaster:	It ________________ get there on time by parcel post, (possibility) but you ________________ be sure by sending it first class. (ability)

4. (At Ruby's Department Store)

Amy:	We ________________ return this sweater. (preference)
Clerk:	You ________________ exchange it for another sweater, or ________________ have a refund? (preference)
Amy:	I ________________ like to exchange it. (possibility) ________________ I look around a little bit? (permission)
Clerk:	Of course you ________________. (permission)

10.3 Modals to Show Obligation

Example Sentences in Context:

Ed: Are you ready to leave for the airport?

Pam: Almost. What time do we *have to* be there?

Ed: At nine. We *must* be there at least an hour before the flight. And it is after eight now.

Pam: *Don't* we *have to* call a cab?

Ed: No, we *don't have to.* George Smith is waiting to drive us there.

Pam: That's great. I'm ready. Let's check on Ann. . . . Ed, can you help Ann? She still *has to* close her suitcase.

(Question Word Order)	Subject	Modal	Verb	Rest of the Sentence
What time do	we	have to	be	there?
	We	must	be	there at nine.
Don't	we	have to	call	a cab?
	We	don't have to.		
	She	has to	close	her suitcase.

Note: *Must* has very strong meaning. *Have to/has to* also show obligation: "You must drive safely." "You have to drive safely. . . ." *Must not* is different. It means *Do not do it:* "You must not throw garbage on the street." *"Mustn't"* is the short form: "You mustn't act so silly." *Don't have to* or *doesn't have to* = there is no obligation: "You don't have to come (if you don't want to)."

You must be on time. = You have to be on time.

You must not be late. ≠ You don't have to be late.

You must *not be late.* = You have to *be on time.*

Exercise 6 You Must Follow the Rules.

Use must *or* must not. *This exercise gives the situation for using* must, *following rules.*

The Springfield High School Driver's Education Course

Andy Garcia is in a special class for driver's education. All students at Springfield High ________________ take this course. They don't have to get a license,

but they ______________ learn about safety on the road. Every student ______________ learn these safe driving rules:

You ______________ always buckle your seat belt.

You ______________ obey the speed limits.

You ______________ slow down on a wet road.

You ______________ signal a turn.

A tired person ______________ drive.

You ______________ drink and drive.

You ______________ stop for pedestrians.

Now write four more rules for safe driving.

____

____

____

____

Exercise 7 A Good Student.

Use must *or* have to *to rewrite the first sentence to mean the same as the first. Change words if necessary. Remember: it might not be possible. (*Doesn't have to *and* must not *do* NOT *mean the same thing.)*

1. A good student has to study. = ______________
2. A good student must do homework. = ______________
3. Good students have to pay attention in class. = ______________
4. Good students must not sleep in class. = ______________
5. A good student doesn't have to stay after school. = ______________

____

Example Sentences in Context:

Kate: I *ought to* study tonight. Dr. Hunter is giving a big math test tomorrow.

Ann: Kate, you *should* try to keep up with your homework.

Kate: I do! I do! But I need an A, so I *had better* review everything. *Shouldn't* you?

Ann: You're right. I *should* too. Let's study together.

Subject	Modal	Verb	Rest of Sentence
I	ought to	study	tonight.
You	should	try	to keep up.
I	had better	review	everything.
I	should	—	too.

Note: The question form for all of these modals is *should.* *Had better* has a short form: *'d better.* (*I'd better* be on time.)

Exercise 8 George and Jerry Talk About the Smith's Model T.

George is giving Jerry some advice about taking care of the car. Use the words in parentheses to complete the sentences.

George: The Model T is a great car, so ________________. (ought to/you/learn to take care of it)

Jerry: Like what, Dad?

George: ________ every week. (check the oil/should/you) You ________ to the radiator frequently. (add water/ought to) And you ________. (should/spark coil/check)

Jerry: And the tires? ________ them every day? (I/should/check) And the windshield? I ________ every day, don't you think? (wash/ought to/it)

George: You ________ down. (calm/had better) You ________ for another two years. (can, drive not)

Exercise 9 It Might Be Possible. Mini-Contexts.

Fill in the blanks with an appropriate model or modal phrase.

1. (At Taylor College, in the Student Advisor's Office)

David Chen: What courses ________ I take? (advisability)

Counselor: Well, you ________ take an English course. (advisability) And you still have a science requirement. You ________ take chemistry, geography, physics, or geology. (advisability)

David Chen: ________? (obligation) This semester I don't have time for a lab.

Counselor: Well, you ________ take a math course and history. (possibility) Those courses are requirements, too. But ________ you ________ take a course in study skills. (obligation) You ________n't register without it. (ability)

David Chen: Well then, I ________________ sign up for English, study skills, math, and history. (ability) ________________ my classes all be in the morning? (possibility)

Counselor: Let's check the schedules. It ________________ be possible. (possibility)

2. (At the Garcia's House)

Rosa: Mama, my throat hurts.

Gloria: Oh honey. ________________ you open your mouth really wide? (ability) ________________ I look at your throat? (permission)

Rosa: No, Mama. I ________________n't open it up wide. (ability) It hurts too much.

Gloria: Well, perhaps we ________________ go to see Dr. Cook. (advisability) She ________________ check your throat and give you some medicine. (possibility)

3. (At Dr. Cook's Office. Mrs. Garcia and Dr. Cook are good friends. They use first names.)

Dr. Cook: Her throat looks really red, Gloria. Perhaps we ________________ check for strep throat. (advisability) And I ________________ take her temperature. (advisability)

Mrs. Garcia: You're the doctor, Shirley. ________________ I keep her out of school for a few days? (advisability)

Dr. Cook: Oh, I don't think so. This medicine ________________ help a lot, and fast. (possibility)

4. (At the Hanson Brothers' Moving Company)

Fred: Tomorrow we move the Baker's furniture to their new house.

Frank: We ________________ call them. (advisability)

Fred: Why don't you do that? I ________________ get some boxes and tape together. (obligation)

Frank: And we ________________ take along a lot of blankets. (advisability) They have a house full of very expensive furniture.

Fred: ________________ we take along some rope? (advisability)

Frank: Yes, rope, blankets, boxes, tape. We ________________ take a lot of everything. (advisability)

10.5 Modals to Show Future Time

Example Sentences in Context:

Sara Walker and Mark Fronski are talking about plans for the hospital.

Dr. Fronski: Springfield *will* probably grow more in the next ten years.

Mrs. Walker: Right! The town *is going to* need more services.

Dr. Fronski: What is your opinion? What *will* the hospital need?

Mrs. Walker: The people in the town *are going to* be older. We probably *won't* need another children's ward.

Dr. Fronski: We *will* probably need a special ward for old people.

Mrs. Walker: How about the emergency room? *Will* we need more space? *Shall* we talk about changes in emergency care with the fire department?

Dr. Fronski: That is a good idea. I*'ll* call them.

(Question Word Order)	Subject	Modal	Verb	Rest of Sentence
	I	'll	call	them.
	We	won't	need	another ward.
	We	will	need	a ward for old people.
	Springfield	will	grow	in the next ten years.
	The town	is going to	need	more services.
What will	the hospital	—	need?	
	The people of Springfield	are going to	be	older.
Will	we	—	need	more space?
Shall	we	—	talk	about it?
	That	would	be	a good idea.

Grammar Notes: Use *shall* only in questions. *Shall* means *Let's* + *?*. The short forms of *will* are *'ll* and *won't*. Use *be going to* to show plans. Use *will* or *'ll* for undecided future. Use *be going to* for plans and *will* to talk about other ideas in the future.

Exercise 10 At the Cafeteria at the Student Union.

Use future markers (will, won't, 'll, BE going to, shall . . . ?).

David Chen: I'm trying to decide on a major. What are you majoring in, John?

John Garcia: I ______________ to be a dentist like my dad.

David: Why do you want to be a dentist?

John: Because I ______________ be able to make good money.

David: But ______________ you be happy?

John: Well, my dad is.

David: Where will you practice?

John: I ______________ share my dad's office. We ___________ be able to have one secretary and a full-time assistant.

David: What dental school ______________ you go to?

John: I ______________ to Northwestern. How about you, David? What are you thinking about?

David: My dad wants me to major in business. My mom thinks computers are great. And I want to be a teacher.

John: ______________ that make you happy?

David: Well, I ______________ not ______________ happy as a businessman, and I don't like computers. I just don't know.

John: Why don't you go to the counseling center? They help a lot of students.

David: That's a good idea. I ______________.

Exercise 11 Football.

Use forms of be going to *or* will *to complete these sentences.*

Gary: ________________ sign up for my football team this year?

Jerry: I'm thinking about it. ________________ you ________________?

Gary: I ________________ ask my mom. She might let me.

Jerry: ________________n't she let you try out?

Gary: Maybe she ________________, and maybe she ________________n't.

Jerry: Maybe she should talk to my mom. She ________________ tell her all about it.

Exercise 12 All Modals. Mini-Contexts.

Add modals to complete these sentences.

1. Kate: I ________________ (future) shopping tomorrow. ________________ (ability) you come with me? I ________________ (requirement) buy a dress for my cousin's wedding.

   Ann: I ________________ (preference) go, but I ________________ (possibility) be working. I ________________ (obligation) check the schedule at the cafeteria.

2. Ed: I don't feel well today. I ________________ (future) stay in bed.

   Pam: ________________ (advisability) I call the doctor?

   Ed: I don't think so. I don't ________________ (preference) drive to his office.

   Pam: I ________________ (possibility) come home at 10:30. I ________________ (possibility) take you.

   Ed: Let me sleep for a while.

   Pam: I ________________ (future) give you a call later.

   Ed: OK.

3. Tony: There's a letter from the voters' registration office. We ________________ (obligation) change our address on our registration.

   Gloria: What ________________ we ________________ (obligation) do?

   Tony: We ________________ (obligation) fill out some forms.

   Gloria: OK. We ________________ (advisability) do it today.

4. Ann: Let's go out to eat.

Bill: Where do you ________________ (preference) go?

Ann: I ________________ (preference) go to Mama Luisa's for pizza.

Bill: That sounds good to me. ________________ (ability) you call Kate and Sue? I ________________ (future) call Tom and Joe. What time (preference) you ________________ go?

Ann: Anytime after six; but I ________________ (requirement) change clothes. I ________________ (possibility) be ready by seven-thirty.

5. Andy: There's a computer class at school this year, but I don't ________________ (preference) take it.

John: Why not? You ________________ (advisability) learn something about computers.

Andy: Why?

John Everyone knows how to use computers. You ________________ (obligation) learn too.

Unit 11: Adjectives

SPRINGFIELD IS A PLEASANT PLACE TO LIVE.

11.1 Positions of Adjectives

Example Sentences in Context:

Jack is *a very good* student. He is *intelligent* and *hard-working.* His *favorite* class is *creative* writing. He hopes to become a writer. Some stories are *good enough* to sell to *popular* magazines, but he's too *practial* to depend on that money. He has his *own tree-planting* business. It is easy enough for a student to handle.

Possessive Adjective/ Demonstrative or Article	Adverb	Adjective	Noun
a	very	good	student
his		favorite	class
a			writer
some			stories
that			money
his own		tree-planting	business

Grammar Note: A noun can have a possessive adjective, (like *her* or *his*), a demonstrative (*this* or *that*), an article (*a, an, the*) or a measure/number word (*some, two, a lot of*). A noun cannot take more than one of these words.

(Too)	Adjective	(Enough)	To Do Something
too	practical		to depend on that
	good	enough	to sell
	easy	enough	for a student

Grammar Note: Use either *too* and adjective or adjective and *enough* with an infinitive phrase (to + verb). These expressions show a cause and effect relationship. *For + a noun* can mean the same thing: His stories are *good enough for magazines.*

Exercise 1 Helping Mrs. Anderson.

Use the words in parentheses to make a sentence.

1. Joe Anderson's grandmother lives next to the Clarks. She lives in ______________________________. (house/pleasant/a)
2. She is ________________ (kind/a/person/very), and all of ________________ (young/the/people) love her very much.
3. Dorothy Anderson is ________________ (listener/a/patient/very), is ________________ (the/kids/neighborhood) gather at ________________ (house/her) after school.
4. She always bakes ________________ (delicious/lots of/cookies/chocolate chip), so the children love to stop there on the way home.
5. Last week Mrs. Anderson had ________________. (accident/very/a/bad). She slipped on ________________ (rug/new/a) and fell.

6. She broke ________________ (left/her/hip) and ________________ (arm/her/right).
7. ________________ (Springfield's/team/rescue) took her to the emergency room. The doctors decided to operate. They put in ________________ (pins/steel/three) to set ________________ (broken/the/bone).
8. Now she is back at home. She can't bake ________________. (wonderful/those/cookies), but the kids still stop at her house after school.
9. Gary and Jerry cut the grass and weed ________________ (garden/her/big/vegetable).
10. Amy and Allison go to visit her on Saturday morning. They clean ________________ (entire/the/house).
11. Ann and Joe go to ________________ (nearby/store/the/grocery) to buy food for Mrs. Anderson.
12. Rosa picks up ________________ (newspaper/Mrs. Anderson's/letters) and takes them to her.
13. Andy waters the lawn and ________________ (the/trees/fruit).
14. Every evening someone brings ________________ (a/delicious/meal/a/home-cooked) to her. Everyone loves Mrs. Anderson.

Exercise 2 Good Enough for Me. Mini-Contexts.

Complete the sentences with the words in parentheses. Use enough *in each blank.*

1. I have a bike. It isn't great, but it's ________________ for me. (good) It goes about fifteen miles an hour. That isn't fast, but that's ________________ for me. (fast) It isn't very pretty, but I don't care. It's ________________ for me. (good)
2. Mrs. Anderson: I have a small house on Fifth Avenue. It has only two bedrooms, but it's ________________ for me. (big) The grocery store is three blocks away. It's ________________ to walk. (close)
3. Amy: Have some lemonade. It's a little sour, but it's ________________ for me. (sweet)

   Ally: Is there some ice? It doesn't look ________________ to drink on a hot day like this. (cold)

4. Ann: Can you hear the music? I can't.
   Bill: Yes, it's ________________ for me to hear, (loud) but I'll turn it up for you.
5. Pam: Here's a cup of coffee. It's ________________ to drink now. (cool)
   Ed: It's also ________________ to wake me up. (strong)
6. Emily: How's the weather today?
   George: It's ________________ to wear a sweater. (cold)
   Emily: Do I need a jacket?
   George: No, by noon it'll be ________________ to go without a sweater. (warm)
7. I'd better not lie down on the couch. I'm ________________ to fall asleep and sleep through my classes. (tired)
8. This road is really narrow. It doesn't look ________________ for two cars. (wide) But there's a lot of traffic. In fact, this road is ________________ for four lanes. (busy) They need a new road, but the town isn't ________________ to build one. (rich)
9. Ricky is only two years old. He isn't ________________ to go to school. (old)
10. I need a box to send these tapes to Germany. This one is ________________ for the tapes (large), but it isn't ________________ to get there in one piece. (strong)

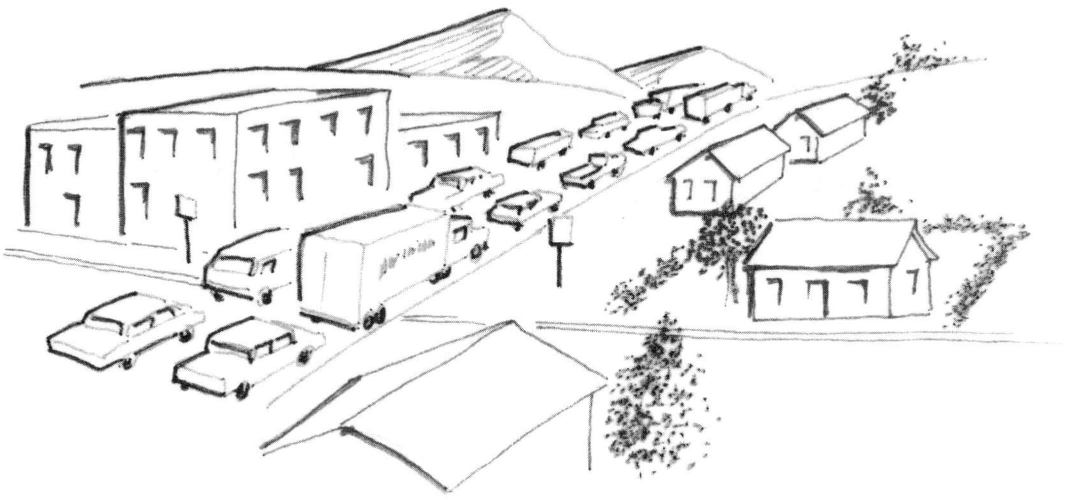

11.2 Making Comparisons

Example Sentences in Context:

Gloria Garcia and Dorothy Anderson live on the same street, but their houses are very different. Gloria's house is *larger* and *more expensive* than Dorothy's. Dorothy's yard is *more beautiful*, and it is *more interesting* than Gloria's. Gloria's house *looks like* a fairy-tale cottage.

Using *-er than* and *more than*			
Gloria's house	is	larger than	Dorothy's house.
Gloria's house	is	more expensive than	Dorothy's house.
It	is	more interesting than	Dorothy's house.

More Example Sentences in Context:

Gloria's house *is similar to* the Smiths' house. In fact, those two houses *are almost alike.* The Garcia's yard *is as big as* the Smiths', but the Smiths' have *older* trees. Dorothy's yard is full of flowers. It's *different from* her neighbors' yards.

Using *like* and *alike*		
It	looks like	a fairy-tale cottage.
The two houses	look alike.	

Using *be* with *similar to, different from, the same as*

Gloria's house	is		similar to	the Smiths'.
The two houses	are	almost	alike.	
Dorothy's yard	is		different from	her neighbors'.
One house	is	almost	the same as	the other.

Spelling Note: To add ***-er*** to an adjective, follow these rules:

▶ **Add *-r* to an adjective with a final e:**

large**r** wide**r** ripe**r** rare**r** loose**r**

▶ **For an adjective ending in *y*, change the *y* to *i* and add *-er:***

eas**ier** earl**ier** heav**ier** friendl**ier** laz**ier**

▶ **For other short (one or two syllables) adjectives, and *-er:***

tall**er** small**er** kind**er** cheap**er** high**er**

▶ **Some adjectives end in a single consonant, but the vowel is short. Double the consonant to add *-er:***

fa**tter** bi**gger** ho**tter** thi**nner** we**tter**

▶ **A few common adjectives are irregular:**

good . . . better This book is good, but that one is better than this one.

bad . . . worse The weather is bad, but yesterday's weather was worse than today's.

▶ **Use *more + adjective* for long adjectives:**

interesting . . . more interesting This book is more interesting than that one.

expensive . . . more expensive This ring is more expensive than the other.

Exercise 3 Which One Is Harder? Mini-Contexts.

Use the comparative form of the underlined adjective.

1. Ann I want to take one <u>easy</u> course next semester, something ________________ than math.

 Bill: What are you thinking about?

 Ann: Oh, maybe chemistry or physics.

 Bill: Physics and chemistry are <u>difficult</u>, Ann. They are ________________ than math.

Ann: Well, math is hard enough. I certainly don't want anything __________ than math. What do you suggest?

Bill: I think geography is simple.

Ann: Is it __________ than geology?

2. The food in the cafeteria is bad; it is even __________ than my mother's cooking. And she burns everything. She makes everything too salty, but cafeteria food is even __________ than my mother's food. Her macaroni and cheese is rubbery, but the cafeteria's is __________ than hers.

3. This popcorn is stale. These potato chips are __________. This brownie is dry, and the cake is even __________. This cheese tastes bad, and these peanuts are __________.

4. The climate in Springfield is pleasant all year round, but it is __________ in the spring than in the winter. It's nice in the summer, but it's __________ in the fall. The air is warm in the spring, but it is __________ in the summer. It's hot in June, but July is even __________. The days are breezy in May, but March is a __________ month.

5. No one has a garden like Dorothy Anderson's. Her long, fresh carrots are __________ and __________ than anyone else's. Her juicy red tomatoes are __________ and __________ than any others in town. Her lettuce is crisp and green. In fact, it is __________ and __________ than anyone else's. The cucumbers from her garden are firm and crunchy. I have never eaten __________ or __________ cucumbers than hers.

6. Parents have a hard job, and it gets ________________ every year. Twenty years ago, kids had to be smart, now they have to be ________________. Before, kids had to have high grades to get into college, now the grades have to be ________________. College was always expensive,* now it's even ________________. Parents always had to be understanding,* but now parents have to be ________________ than ever before. (*Use *more,* not -er.)
7. When Ricky Smith was born, the family was happy, but they were even ________________ when Emily came home with the new baby. Her skin is soft, but the baby's skin was even ________________. Jerry was a tiny baby, but Ricky was even ________________. Peggy was a sweet baby, but Ricky was even ________________.
8. Other hair stylists are good, but Max is ________________ than any other hair stylist in town. Some of them cut hair in straight lines, but Max cuts hair even ________________ than they do. Some give a wavy permanent, but Max's perms are ________________. Some hair stylists trim close, but Max trims even ________________.

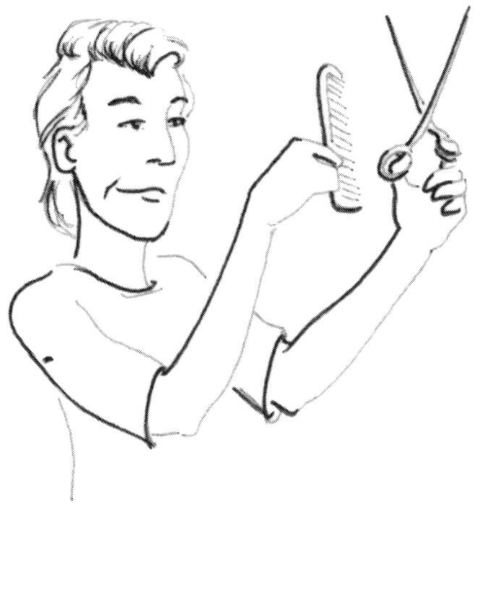

Exercise 4 The Twins.

Use like, alike, similar to, different from, *or* the same as *to complete these sentences.*

1. Amy and Allison Walker are twins, so their faces are ________________. Amy's hair is ________________ than Allison's because Amy's hair is short and Ally's is long. Allison chooses clothes ________________ her mother's, but Amy always wears clothes ________________ theirs.
2. Ally's study habits are ________________ from her sister's. She studies at the library ________________ Ann Clark. Amy doesn't. She studies ________________ most teenagers at the last minute, just before a test.
3. Both twins are very friendly. They are ________________ in their friendliness, but Allison is ________________ Amy. Amy talks a lot, and Ally is quiet. Their brother Gary is ________________ Amy. He talks a lot too.
4. Because the girls look ________________, their teachers have trouble telling them apart. In a few weeks, however, they learn. Amy's personality is ________________ her sister's. Ally's grades are usually higher. She is serious ________________ her father. She is hard working ________________ her mother. Amy is ________________ her mother's sister, a fun-lover.

Exercise 5 Write About Yourself.

Complete these sentences and use comparative adjectives.

I look like ________________. My hair is similar to ________________. I am different from my family in some important ways. I am different from my mother because I am ________________. I am different from my dad because I am ________________. I am the same as ________________ because I am ________________.

Example Sentences in Context:

Vote for Joe Anderson! Joe is the *friendliest* man on campus. He is the *most intelligent* student and the *most honest* person in the junior class. Vote for Joe! He's the *best*!

The	(Most)	Adjective (-est)	Noun	(Of All)
the	—	friendliest	man	on campus
the	most	intelligent	student	
the	most	honest	person	in the class
the		best		

Note: Use the *-est* form with short adjective (1 or 2 syllables). Use *the most* with long adjectives.

Exercise 6 Vote for Joe!

Use the adjective in parentheses to complete the sentence. Remember to use the. *Use* the most, *if necessary.*

Ann: Why should I vote for Joe Anderson?

Bill: Well, Joe is ________________ candidate. (dependable) Joe is ________________ too. (cooperative) He is ________________ (hard-working), so he'll work hard for all of us students. Besides that, Joe is ________________ (friendly) and he is ________________ (sensitive) to the needs of students. Joe is ________________ (good) listener. Besides that, he is ________________ (handsome) of all the candidates.

Ann: OK. I'll vote for Joe.

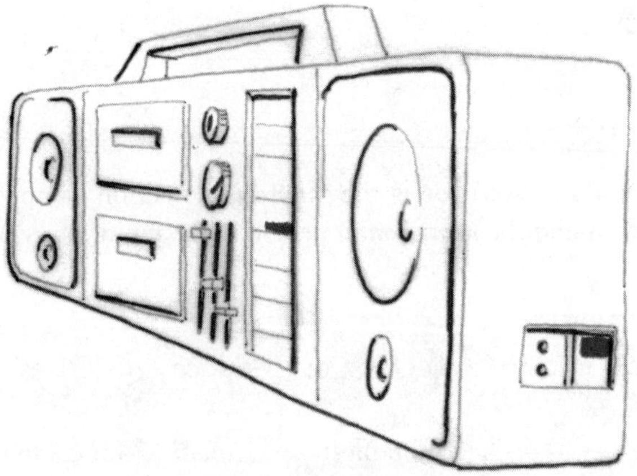

Exercise 7 It's the Most! Mini-Contexts.

Rewrite the underlined sentences to include a superlative adjective. Add expressions like of all.

1. Buy a BIG BLASTER! It gives clear sound. It is light. It is a loud radio. It has good speakers. The price of a BIG BLASTER is reasonable. ______________________
____
____
____

2. Visit Spooky Shadows, the Haunted House. It has a dark entrance. There are strange sounds in the house. There are weird pictures on the wall. It is a scary place.
____
____
____

3. Mrs. Garcia is a great teacher. She is patient, and she is kind. She is an interesting person too. She has a funny sense of humor. ______________________________

____

____

____

4. Springfield General is an efficient hospital. There is a good staff of doctors and nurses. They have new equipment. The ambulance service is fast. ______________________________

____

____

____

5. Tom Turner and Joe Anderson run every morning. They want to be in good shape. They are early risers in the dorm. Tom thinks that 5 A.M. is a good time to run.

____

____

____

6. Ruby's Department Store is large. They have a wide selection of clothes. They sell beautiful and expensive dresses for women. They also have a great variety of tools, furniture, and toys. ______________________________

____

____

____

7. Shirley Cook is a fine doctor. She was a smart student in her class. She earned high grades and won a big scholarship. Shirley is a hard-worker, and she is friendly. She is popular with the patients. ______________________________

____

____

____

8. Jason Walker runs an efficient electronics factory. He is successful at TTT. He is an outgoing person, so he is an important executive for the company. ______________________________

____

____

____

Example Sentences in Context:

Ann: Let's go! This movie is boring.

Bill: No, I like it. It's interesting.

Ann: I want to go! I'm bored.

Bill: But I want to stay! I'm interested. It's not a boring movie. Maybe you just don't understand it.

Noun	(BE)	Verbal Adjective
This movie	is	boring.
It	's	interesting.
I	'm	bored.
I	'm	interested.

(Verbal Adjective)	Noun
a boring	movie

Grammar Note: In the sentence "This movie is boring" the word *boring* comes from the verb *to bore.* The movie "does" the *boring*; the movie causes the feeling of boredom (being bored). Therefore, "I am bored."

All verbal adjectives come from verbs: "The movie bores me" is the basic sentence. The subject noun takes the verbal adjective with *-ing*: "The movie is boring." The object noun (me) changes to become a subject (I). Then the *-ed* form can modify the noun. ("I am bored.")

Exercise 8 What a Movie!

Complete the sentences to use the underlined verb as the -ing *form and the* -ed *form.*

1. The movie excited everyone in the audience. The movie was ________________. Everyone in the audience was ________________.
2. The actor amused us all. The actor was ________________. We were all ________________.
3. The plot thrilled the people in the theater. The people in the theater were ________________. The plot was ________________.

4. The ending surprised me. I was ________________ by the ending. The ending was ________________ to me.
5. The movie didn't disappoint me. I wasn't ________________. The movie wasn't ________________.
6. The movie tired us all. We were all ________________ by the movie. The movie was ________________.
7. The message of the film confused the audience. I was ________________ by the message. The message of the movie was ________________.
8. The whole production amazed us. We were ________________. The whole production was ________________.

Exercise 9 It's Amazing! Mini-Contexts.

Rewrite the sentences to use the -ing *or* -ed *form of the underlined word.*

1. Exercise tires me out.

   ____

   Jogging bores me.

   ____

   Feeling fit pleases me.

   ____

2. This book interests the junior high school students.

   ____

   The plot amuses them.

   ____

   The style confuses them sometimes.

   ____

   The high point of the story shocks them.

   ____

3. The speech convinced me about the election.

____

The speaker fascinated all of us in the audience.

____

His stories amazed us.

____

4. The hike tired me.

____

The hike exhausted me.

____

The climb frightened me.

____

5. That story disgusted me.

____

It disappointed me.

____

The ending shocked me.

____

The whole experience confused me.

____

6. The haunted house frightened the children.

____

The haunted house amazed them.

____

The haunted house surprised the little ones.

____

Example Sentences in Context:

Amy: Take a sweater! It's very cold outside. It's too cold for short sleeves.
Ally: Is it really cold? Or just cool?
Amy: Well, it's somewhat colder than last night. It's too cold to go out for a walk.

Modifier	Adjective	
very	cold	
too	cold	for short sleeves
too	cold	to go out for a walk
really	cold	
somewhat	colder	than last night

Note: These words are modifiers. They change the meaning of the adjective. The weather can be . . .

a little	cold	
rather	cold	
somewhat	cold	
quite	cold	
really	cold	
very	cold	
extremely	cold	
too	cold	to do something
not	cold	at all

Exercise 10 About Me.

Answer these question about you.

1. How tall are you? I'm ________________ tall.

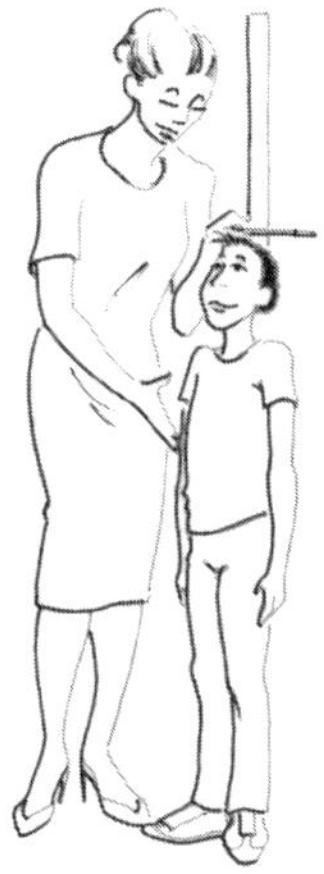

2. How good a student are you? I'm __________ good as a student.
3. How intelligent are you? I'm __________ intelligent.
4. How interesting are your stories? My stories are __________ interesting.
5. How good-looking are you? I'm __________ good-looking.
6. How interesting are you as a conversation partner? I am __________ as a talker.
7. How interested are you in boats? I'm __________ in boats.
8. How happy are you now? I'm __________ happy now.

Exercise 11 How's the Weather?

Complete these sentences with modifiers.

1. Last summer the weather was __________ hot.
2. The days were __________ humid too.
3. The rain was __________ plentiful.
4. Last fall the weather was __________ breezy.
5. The nights were __________ cold.
6. The days were __________ warm and sunny.
7. The winter was also __________ pleasant.
8. The days were __________ pleasant.

Exercise 12 I Couldn't Do It.

Complete the sentences with good excuses.

1. I couldn't read the lesson. I was too __________.
2. I didn't take the quiz. I was too __________.
3. I didn't do my homework. I was too __________.
4. I couldn't call you last night. I was too __________.
5. I wasn't able to help you. I was too __________.
6. Sally broke her leg. She was too __________.
7. Sally can't ski any more. She is too __________.
8. Sally is afraid. She is too __________.

Unit 12: Adverbs

THEY WERE IN SPRINGFIELD TWO YEARS AGO.

12.1 Adverbs of Time

Example Sentences in Context:

I was born here *eighteen years ago.*

My birthday was *in December.*

I was born *when my mother was twenty-five years old.*

I live in Springfield *now.*

We lived in the city *for a few years,* but *then* we moved back.

Time Adverb	Sentence	Time Adverb
	I live in Springfield	now.
	We lived in the city	for a few years,
but then	we moved back.	
	I was born here	eighteen years ago.
	My birthday was	in December.
	I was born	when my mother was 25 years old.

Grammar Note: A time adverb can be at the beginning or end of the sentence. It can be a single word (now, then), a phrase (eighteen years ago, in December), or a clause (when my mother was 25 years old).

Exercise 1 They'll Do It Then. Mini-Contexts.

Rewrite these sentences. Put the adverb in a different place in the sentence.

1. The Walkers lived in Chicago last year. Mrs. Walker worked at a large downtown hospital until a month ago. They moved to Springfield then. ______________________

____

____

____

____

2. Jason Walker went to New York a month ago. He also went to New Orleans last year. He went to Toronto last summer. He took a business trip to Tokyo recently. He is at home today. He leaves on another trip tomorrow. ____________________

3. Ann Clark is taking Math 101 this semester. She got good grades last semester. She is afraid of geeting low grades now. She has a big test in the morning. She will study a lot tonight. ____________________

4. Yesterday Tom ran five miles. Today he ran five more. Tomorrow he plans to run five more miles. In a week he will be in a race. ____________________

5. Ed Clark teaches in the morning. In the afternoon he has office hours. He goes to play golf on some Saturdays. This week Ed is in a tennis tournament. ____________________

Exercise 2 When?

Combine these pairs of sentences. Turn the answer to the question into a time adverb phrase or clause.

Example: (When did you start school?) I started school when I was five years old.

1. (When did you learn to walk?)
   I learned to walk when ____________________.
2. (When did you start to talk?)
   I started to talk when ____________________.
3. (When did you get your first haircut?)
   I got my first haircut when ____________________.

4. (When did you take your first trip?)
   I took my first trip when ______________________________.

5. (When did you learn to ride a bicycle?)
   I learned to ride a bicycle when ______________________________.

6. (When did you first earn some money?)
   ____

7. (When did you get a real job?)
   ____

8. (When did you start learning English?)
   ____

12.2 Adverbs of Place

Example Sentences in Context:

Where did I put my purse? I put it *here*, but it's not *here* now. Did I put it *in the closet*? No, it's not *there*. It must be *someplace*. Oh, here it is, *on my arm*. That's *where I always put it*.

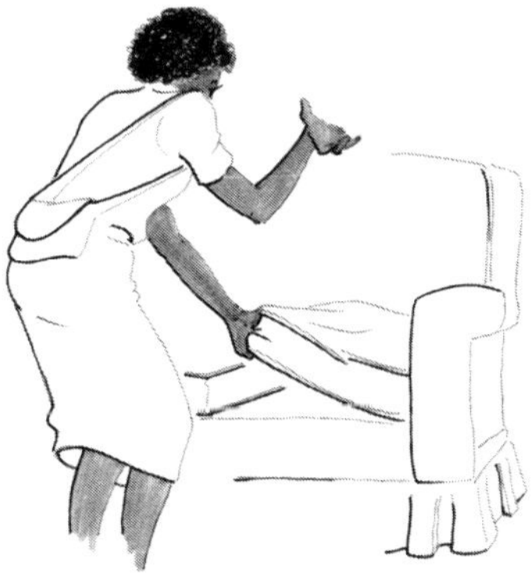

Question Word Order

Question Word	Helping Verb	Subject	Verb	Adverb of Place
Where	did	I	put my purse?	
		I	put it	here.
		It	's not	here now.
	Did	I	put it	in the closet?
		It	must be	someplace.
		It	's	on my arm.
		That	's	where I put it.

Grammar Note: Adverbs of place usually come at the end of a sentence. Adverbs of place can be single words *(where, here, there)*, phrases *(in the closet, on my arm)*, or clauses *(where I always put it)*. Adverbs of time usually follow place adverbs: *here now.*

Exercise 3 Where Am I? Where Is It?

Fill in the blanks. Use the cue words and follow special directions. Add the preposition. For example, in number 1, write the names of the country and city where you are.

A: Where am I?

B: I'm _in the United States_ (country) _in Flagstaff, Arizona_ (city).

1. A Where am I?

   B: I'm ______________ (country) ______________ (city).

2. A: Where is the weather hot now?

   B: ______________ (state or country).

3. A: It's daytime here. Where is it nighttime?

   B: ______________, ______________, and ______________. (3 countries)

4. A: Where did I put my backpack?

   B: Is it ______________ ______________ ______________?

   A: No, I looked ______________.

   B: Is it ______________ ______________ ______________?

   Or ______________ ______________ ______________?

   A: No, I think it's lost. I've looked ______________.

   B: ______________ it is!

   A: ______________ was it? Right ______________, under our noses.

   B: Right! Under the newspaper, your jacket, and this pile of magazines.

Grammar Note: When there are two adverbs of time or place, there is often a question of which one should come first. The principle is to put the smaller first unless the other is more important.

If one part (for example, the day) is more important than another (like the time), the natural choice for first is the day: Tuesday at three o'clock.

If the two elements are equally important, most people put the smaller one first: at seven o'clock on Friday.

The time (7 o'clock) is a smaller unit than a day (Friday).

If the time adverb is a length of time, it is usually second: on Friday morning from 8 to 12.

If there are two place adverbs, put the more important one first: at home in bed.

If the two adverbs are equally important, then put the smaller unit first: at home in Wisconsin.

Put the place adverbs before the time adverbs: at home this evening.

Exercise 4 What's Happening, Where, and When?

This Week in Springfield.

At the high school:	At the mall:	At the country club:
Springfield vs. Midlands Football Friday, 7 PM Memorial Stadium **Debate Tournament** Fri., Sat., Sun., 7 PM Bradley Auditorium	**Car Show** All day, Monday through Saturday **Arts and Crafts** All day, Saturday, Sunday, Monday	**Celebrity Golf Tournament** All day Saturday **Celebrity Ball** Saturday, 9 PM
At the airport:	**At Taylor College:**	**At the movies:**
Open House Saturday, 9 PM to 5 PM New Terminal Building	**Tennis match** Thursday, 2 PM College Courts **Speaker: Dr. Hans Schmidt on "Back to Basics"** Thursday, 5 PM Taylor Hall	**Downtown Cinema** **"Monsters of the Deep"** Shows at 7 PM and 9 PM weekdays and at 3 PM, 5 PM, 7 PM, 9 PM weekends **Movies-at-the-Mall** **"Trouble on the Horizon"** Daily 2 PM, 4 PM, 6 PM, 8 PM

Answer the questions using the schedule above, "This Week in Springfield."

Example: A: What's happening at the airport this week?
B: There is an open house *at the new terminal building on Saturday from 9–5 PM.*

(A is reading the newspaper)

1. Ed: Springfield High School is certainly a busy place.
   Pam: Oh? What's going on there?
   Ed: Well, there's a football game ______________________ ______________________ (where, when).
2. Ed: There's a debate tournament too. It's ______________________ ______________________ (where, when).
3. Pam: Isn't there a play this week too?
   Ed: Yes. The Drama Club is putting on "The Importance of Being Earnest" ______________________ (where, when).

4. Pam: Is there anything going on at Taylor College?

Ed: Let me see. Yes, there's a lecture ____ (where, when).

Pam: Who is speaking?

Ed: Hans Schmidt, on "Back to Basics."

5. Pam: Are there any exciting sports events?

Ed: There's a tennis match ____________________ (when).

Pam: Oh? Where?

Ed: ____.

6. Pam: Let's go to the mall.

Ed: Now?

Pam: Sure, there's a car show ____________________ (where, when).

7. Ed: What else is going on at the mall?

Pam: There's a movie ____.

8. Ed: There's an art show too.

Pam: Where?

Ed: ____.

Pam: When?

Ed: ____.

9. Pam: Let's go to the Country Club this weekend.

Ed: OK. There's a Celebrity Golf Tournament ____.

Pam: Oh, is that this weekend?

Ed: Yes, and ____________________ a Celebrity Ball. Do you want to go?

Pam: Let's!

10. Ed: Just for your information.

Pam: Yes?

Ed: "Monsters of the Deep" is playing ____.

12.3 Adverbs of Manner

Example Sentences in Context:

Sara is a very *quiet* person. She even talks *quietly*. She is always *polite*. She even complains *politely*. She is a *good* talker. She runs meetings *well*.

Adjective		Adverb
A *quiet*	person talks	*quietly.*
A *polite*	person can even complain	*politely.*
A *good*	talker runs meetings	*well.*

Grammar Note: Some adverbs describe *how*. The adjective *good* has an unusual form for its adverb, *well*. The adjective describes a person, but this kind of adverb describes an action. The name for these adverbs is adverbs of manner. These adverbs come from adjectives. Most of them end in *-ly*.

A few common adverbs (from adjectives) do not change at all:

early: The *early* mail comes *early.*
fast: A *fast* driver goes *fast.*
hard: I study *hard* for a *hard* test.
late: The *late* bus leaves really *late.*

Exercise 5 Sara Works Efficiently. Mini-Contexts.

Change the underlined adjective into an adverb and complete the sentence.

1. "I'll write a quick note to my mother," Sara said. And she wrote one ________________.
2. Sara is a careful writer. She writes all the words ________________.
3. She is also a fast writer. She can write ________________.
4. Sara is a very neat person. She writes ________________, and she dresses ________________ too.

5. Being a hospital administrator is a hard job. Sara works ________________.

6. She is a good administrator. She does her job ________________.

7. She is an early riser. She gets to work ________________.

8. She is never late for work, but she often works ________________.

9. Sara is always clear in her directions to hospital staff. She writes ________________.

10. Her hospital is an efficient one. She runs it ________________.

Exercise 6 I Can See Clearly. Mini-Contexts.

Use the adjective in parentheses to form the adverb form. Complete the sentences with the adverb.

1. I can see ________________ (clear) now.
   I can answer your questions ________________ (careful) too.
   I can speak English ________________ (fluent).

2. It's easy to listen to Dr. Hunter in class. He speaks so ________________ (good). He explains the math problems ________________ (clear). He returns homework ________________ (fast). He is an ideal teacher.

3. Because she is a lawyer, Pam needs to be able to speak ________________ (loud) and ________________ (clear). Sometimes in court she must speak ________________ (forceful). She works ________________ (hard) at her job as lawyer.

4. The woman at the piano played ________________ (soft). Her fingers moved ________________ (slow) over the keys. Her body moved ________________ (gentle) back and forth with the music.

5. In court a person must always speak ________________ (truthful). A witness must tell his or her story ________________ (honest). She or he must relate all details ________________ (clear).
6. The man on the television program answered the question ________________ (correct). He won $10,000! He smiled ________________ (broad), and then he ________________ (quick) shook the hands of all the people. He took the check and left the TV studio ________________ (fast).
7. The old man waited ________________ (patient) at the corner of two busy streets. The cars passed by ________________ (dangerous). Then a young woman came to the corner. She turned her head ________________ (slow) toward the old man and spoke ________________ (soft) to him. He nodded his head, she took his arm ________________ (firm), and they waited. The traffic light changed, and the two walked ________________ (direct) across the street.

8. The young woman waited for the job interview ________________ (eager). In the reception room she walked back and forth ________________ (nervous). She seemed to be talking to someone in her head. Then the secretary called her. "Mr. Scott will see you now," he said. The young woman smiled ________________ (warm) and walked ________________ (confident) into the office.

9. Sam unloaded the meat from the truck ________________ (fast). He looked at his watch ________________ (quick). Sam was behind schedule. There were so many boxes to carry into the steakhouse that he was ________________ (late). He worked ________________ (tireless) to stay on schedule.

10. The car swerved ________________ (dangerous) on the ice road. The driver slowed down ________________ (cautious). He pulled off the road ________________ (careful).

More Example Sentences in Context:

Sara runs the hospital *in her own efficient way*. She treats her employees *like members of a family*. She makes decisions *with the good of all* in her mind.

Grammar Note: Not all adverbs of manner are single words. Sometimes prepositional phrases are adverbs of manner.

(*How* does Sara run the hospital?)	*In her own efficient way.*
(*How* does she treat her employees?)	*Like members of a family.*
(*How* does she make decisions?)	*With the good of all in mind.*

Exercise 7 Treat Everyone with Respect. Mini-Contexts.

Rewrite the sentence using a prepositional phrase in place of the single underlined adverb. Use "in a ________________ manner" or a phrase of your own. (with, in *and* for *are useful prepositions.)*

1. Treat everyone respectfully. ________________________________
2. Always dress neatly. ________________________________
3. Speak directly and sincerely. ________________________________
4. Offer to help needy people gently. ________________________________
5. Talk quietly but distinctly. ________________________________

6. Give directions firmly and clearly. ______
7. Give your opinions honestly. ______
8. Give your advice tactfully. ______
9. Try to help quickly. ______
10. Follow the rules exactly. ______

Exercise 8 How Should a Person Talk?

Answer these questions for yourself.

1. How do you like to be treated? ______
2. How should a person dress? ______
3. How should a person speak to others? ______
4. How should a person offer help to needy people? ______
5. How should a person talk? ______
6. How should a person give directions to others? ______
7. How should a person give opinions? ______
8. How should a person give advice? ______
9. How should a person try to help? ______
10. How should a person follow the rules? ______

12.4 Clauses as Adverbs of Manner

Example Sentences in Context:

A: He looks *the way you look.*
He runs *the way you run.*
He talks *the way you talk.*
He tells jokes *the way you do.*
Do you know him?

B: Yes. He's my son.

Grammar Note: A phrase-clause like "the way you look" is also an adverb of manner. It tells *how* a person does something.

Exercise 9 The Way You Do. Mini-Contexts.

Example: A: How do you tie a knot?

B: *The same way you do.*

A: How do you untie a knot?

B: *The way Alexander the Great did,* with a knife.

1. A: How do you study for math?

   B: ________________ Dr. Hunter ________________.

   A: How does Dr. Hunter say to prepare for the test?

   B: ________________ he ________________, by studying the principles.

2. A: How does a child learn to talk?

   B: ________________ his parents ________________.

   A: How does a child act?

   B: ________________ his friends ________________.

3. A: How does a dog behave?

   B: ________________ it owner trains ________________.

   A: How does a puppy behave?

   B: ________________ it wants to!

4. A: How does an actor act?

   B: ________________ the director ________________.

   A: How does an actor in a play dress?

   B: ________________ the director ________________.

5. A: How do you swim?

   B: ____

   A: How do you dance?

   B: ____

   A: How do you exercise?

   B: ____

Exercise 10 Just Like His Dad. Mini-Contexts.

Rewrite the sentences. Use either "like you" (or another person) or "the same way you do." Use appropriate nouns and verbs for each situation.

1. a. You and your dad look alike.

   ____

b. You both dress in wild colors.

___

c. The two of you laugh alike.

___

2. You and your mother are alike in these ways:

a. hair style

___

b. smile

___

c. eye color

___

d. sense of humor

___

3. a. Gary and his dad Jason are alike. They look alike.

___

b. They both enjoy riding bicycles.

___

c. They are both good athletes.

___

d. They both love strawberry ice cream and Chinese food.

___

4. Joe Anderson and his grandmother are a lot alike.

a. They both like to be outdoors.

___

b. They both enjoy reading.

___

c. They are both very friendly people.

___

d. They both have lots of friends.

___

5. Ricky and Jerry are brothers. Ricky wants to be just like Jerry. He likes the way . . .

   a. Jerry plays with a basketball.

   ____

   b. Jerry climbs trees.

   ____

   c. Jerry rides his bicycle.

   ____

   d. Jerry sits and reads.

   ____

   e. Jerry plays games on the computer.

   ____

6. Ricky wants to . . .

   a. Jerry plays with a basketball.

Example: *Ricky wants to play with a basketball the way Jerry does.*

   b. Jerry climbs trees.

   ____

   c. Jerry rides his bicycle.

   ____

   d. Jerry sits and reads.

   ____

   e. Jerry plays games on the computer.

   ____

Example Sentences in Context:

A: Anything you can do I can do better.
I can do anything *better than you.*
I can ride my bicycle *faster.*
I can read more *efficiently than you can.*
I can talk more *fluently.*

B: Oh yes? Well, I'm a *better student than you.*
In fact, I'm *the best student in my class.*
And I can run *the fastest of all.*
I can read *the most efficiently.*
I can spell *the best too.*

A: I wonder which of us brags *more.*

B: I think you brag *the most of all.*

A: I think two terrific people like us should be friends.

Subject	Verb Phrase	Comparative Adverb Phrase
I	can do anything	better than you.
I	can ride my bicycle	faster.
I	can read	more efficiently than you can.
I	can talk	more fluently.
Which of us	brags	more?

Subject	Verb Phrase	Superlative Adverb Phrase
I	can run	the fastest of all.
I	can read	the most efficiently.
I	can spell	the best.
Which of us	brags	the most?

Grammar Note: Comparatives (*more* or *-er*) are used for two people; you are comparing two. Superlative forms are used for more than two (because—of the group—one is the best, the worst, the most . . .).

Exercise 11 My Parents Are the Greatest.

Use the adverb in parentheses in either the comparative or superlative form. Decide according to the context.

I'd like to be just like my parents. For example, my dad is ________________ (patient) of all the dads I know. He is not only the nicest person, but he also tells jokes ________________ (good). He and Jerry's dad are a lot alike, but my dad plays basketball ________________ (good). Jerry's dad works hard, but my dad works ________________ (hard). Besides all that, my dad thinks ________________ (clear) of all the dads in the world! My mother is also the greatest! She makes pizza ________________ (fast) and ________________ (good) than any cook in any pizza place. She takes ________________ (good) care of me than anyone else. She acts ________________ (cool) of all the moms of my friends. She also makes ________________ (good) decisions of all moms. For example, last night she decided that we should all go to Disneyland.

Exercise 12 Well, Better, the Best. Mini-Contexts.

Rewrite these sentences two times. Change the adverb into a comparative and then write the sentence again with a superlative form.

1. a. Tom Turner is a track star. He runs *fast.*

   ____

   ____

   b. Tom is a long distance runner. He jogs *steadily.*

   ____

   ____

   c. Tom practices *consistently.*

   ____

   ____

   d. Tom trains *regularly.*

   ____

   ____

2. a. Dorothy bakes cookies *well.*

   ____

   ____

b. She talks *naturally* with young people.

____

____

c. She listens *carefully* to their problems.

____

____

d. She advises them *honestly.*

____

____

3. a. Dr. Hunter teaches math *effectively.*

____

____

b. His students learn *efficiently.*

____

____

c. They learn math principles *thoroughly.*

____

____

d. They get good grades *consistently.*

____

____

c. They understand math *completely.*

____

____

4. a. The roads are icy tonight. Please drive *safely*.

b. Drive *slowly*.

c. Watch for other cars *carefully*.

d. Cross intersections *cautiously*.

5. a. Have you heard Ed Clark? He talks *loudly*.

b. He also sings *well*.

c. He speaks French, Spanish, and Italian *fluently*.

d. In class he lectures *naturally*.

e. He answers questions *easily*.

Exercise 13 All Adverbs.

Many sentences have more than one adverb. The usual place for an adverb is at the end of a sentence. However, adverbs can appear in several places (at the beginning of the sentence, at the end, and—in the case of adverbs of frequency—in the middle.) It is natural to put most time adverbs first in the sentence.

Example:

I *often* see you *in your office quickly in the morning.*
frequency place manner time

In the morning I *often* see you *quickly in your office.*
time frequency manner place

Arrange the elements for these sentences to make good and interesting sentences.

Part A

1. [students work] (at the beginning of a school year/very hard/in their classes/usually)

____

____

2. [they read all the assignments] (quickly/after each class/always)

____

____

3. [some students use tape recorders] (sometimes/openly/in their lectures)

____

____

4. [they go to their rooms to listen to the lectures again] (after class/immediately)

5. [students continue taping] (rarely/after a few weeks)

6. [they start taking good notes] (in class/then/frequently)

7. [they learn an important lesson] (gradually/usually/at this time/in college classes)

8. [pay attention and take notes] (in a university class/always/efficiently)

9. [listen; it may be your only opportunity to hear it] (carefully/in class)

10. [read everything as if it's your only chance] (for a class/thoroughly/always)

Part B

1. [I went shopping] (yesterday/in the afternoon/at the mall/by myself)

2. [I went through many stores] (slowly/before three o'clock)

3. [I couldn't find anything to buy] (for three hours/in the stores)

4. [I went to the Hanger] (unhappily/then)

5. [I found everything] (happily/there/at the Hanger)

Index

To use this index, note the following:

Bold arabic numbers indicate units.
Regular arabic numbers indicate page numbers.
Unit sections devoted to grammar explanations are given in parentheses.
Words and expressions are underlined; grammatical items and headings are not.

N

O

P

Q

R